RELATIONSHIPS IN EARLY CHILDHOOD:

Helping Young Children Grow

RELATIONSHIPS
IN EARLY CHILDHOOD:

Helping Young Children Grow

ERNA FURMAN

INTERNATIONAL UNIVERSITIES PRESS, INC.

Madison   Connecticut

Relationships in Early Childhood: Helping Young Children Grow
(ISBN 0-8236-8272-2)

The Library of Congress has catalogued the hardcover edition of this book as follows:

Library of Congress Cataloging in Publication Data

Furman, Erna.
  Helping young children grow.

  Bibliography: p.
  Includes index.
  1. Child development. I. Title.
HQ767.9.F87   1987   649'.1   87-3196
ISBN 0-8236-2322-X

Manufactured in the United States of America

Contents

Preface

This paperback edition of *Helping Young Children Grow* (E. Furman, 1987a) differs from the earlier hardback in two respects: (1) It is divided into three volumes, representing Parts I, II, and III in the original, and accordingly titled *Relationships in Early Childhood, Self-Control and Mastery in Early Childhood* (E. Furman, 1998b), and *Needs, Urges, and Feelings in Early Childhood* (E. Furman, 1998a). The aim is to allow the reader to begin by focusing on the area of his or her special interest. (2) The references and related reading sections are updated.

    The Teacher's Guide to Helping Young Children Grow (E. Furman, 1987b), the companion book to the original edition, remains available as an important aid to those who are interested in using any or all volumes of *Helping Young Children Grow* as a textbook in teaching a child development–parenting course. This is the purpose for which the book was initially designed, and it has been used successfully with groups as diverse as high school, college, and medical students; educators and mental health professionals at all levels; parents of all ages; and, not least, teachers learning to teach such a course.

    The Teacher's Guide also describes how *Helping Young Children Grow* developed as a project of the Cleveland Center for Research in Child Development, the work of the research group, and the source and use of the data, that is, the scientific basis of the book. Beginning in 1974, the research group consisted of Elizabeth Daunton, Eleanor Fiedler, Robert A. Furman, M.D., Joan Rich, Ph.D., Arthur L Rosenbaum, M.D., and myself. I am most appreciative of and thankful for the contributions of my colleagues. My gratitude extends also to

Penny Friedman and Theodore B. Wiehe, Jr., the first teachers trained to teach this Child Development course. Their experiences and those of their students helped shape the final format and content of the book.

January 1998   Erna Furman

Introduction: How We Learn About Child Development

We learn most things either by taking in previously unknown facts or by marshaling what we already know within ourselves and thinking it through in such a way as to reach a new level of understanding. With both methods, the relationship with the teacher and his or her influence as a model play an important role. With the first way of learning, the teacher presents new facts; with the second way, he or she assists us in developing our own thinking—the Socratic method. In dialogues, Socrates' pupils struggled to formulate their ideas and he, as teacher, questioned their evidence, reasoning, and conclusions to help them note their mistakes and refine their understanding. The special enjoyment and sense of inner conviction we derive from this form of learning has not been lost through the millenia. Most of us can recall some experience with it and know how good it feels. One high school senior, participating in one of our child development courses, put it this way: "What I learned today was especially meaningful because I knew it for the first time, and yet it had been with me all along and been part of my daily experience without me realizing it."

In practice we usually combine both methods of learning. However well we utilize, and are helped to utilize, the knowledge that already lies within us, we still need to add new facts from without. However eager we are to take in new facts, to make them truly our own, we still need to fit them in with what we already know, so that new and old knowledge become a coherent whole and can serve us as a base for further

1

understanding and mastery. With some subjects, such as reading, history, and mathematics, we primarily tend to acquire new facts because, at least initially, we know little or nothing about them. Even in these fields, however, effective learning increasingly depends on our ability to use and develop what we know, to integrate new facts into our existing inner framework, and to build on it. Other subjects, and child development is among them, can never be learned simply by taking in new facts. One reason for this is that we are not novices. All of us have, through our own experiences, accumulated a body of knowledge in this field. Another reason is that this subject calls not only upon our intellect, but also involves our feelings, attitudes, and values. These have, in individual ways, molded our intellectual perception and understanding of child development in the past, and they continue to exercise a special influence on any additional learning we undertake.

In learning about child development, therefore, it is very necessary to draw on our available knowledge and to use it to develop and formulate our own better understanding. It is just as necessary to add new facts in a manner and at a pace which allow us to integrate them effectively.

This is not always easy. Insofar as the new facts are in accord with what we already think, feel, and know, we assimilate them readily. They are not totally foreign and may merely extend or deepen our prior knowledge. But when the new facts run counter to our own ideas, when they seem quite strange, and may even be felt as a threat, we cannot fit them into our own framework. How do our minds cope with this hurdle?

One way is to bury, or set aside, in ourselves all that we know, feel, and think, and to take in eagerly all the new knowledge that is available. We pile the newly presented facts on top of our previous experience without making the necessary inner confrontations and connections. But the new knowledge never truly becomes a part of ourselves. It remains isolated in our minds, fails to advance our real understanding, and cannot be applied to solving problems. We tend to forget it after a while, or set it aside as useless, and we look for a "newer," different body of knowledge, or we make do without. Gradually the old buried experience resurfaces and takes over the void. Most of us can recall taking a class in which we crammed in long lectures and whole bookfuls of new facts, but since we could never integrate them into our own life experience, we can now recover only meaningless relics or muddled dicta. Such has been the fate of many an erudite course or book on child development.

Another way is to reject the new, uncongenial facts outright in favor of our own knowledge. Freud said that education, government, and psychoanalysis—and we may add child development—comprise the most difficult professions because so many people consider themselves experts on the basis of their limited personal experience. All of us have indeed been educated and governed, and have experienced inner stress and turmoil. Most of us have also educated others, governed their lives to some extent, and helped them with their troubles, as parents, relatives, baby-sitters, friends, or even in one or another professional capacity. Regardless of whether we fared well or poorly, these experiences have been such an intimate part of our lives for as long as we can remember that we are apt to view them as a qualifying certificate. Sometimes we even believe that people are naturally endowed with expertise in these fields. Many a young mother and father have been too ashamed to admit their panicky helplessness in figuring out what their baby was crying for, or how to comfort him, because they thought that all other parents knew naturally the right thing to do. After all, "anybody knows what to do with a little kid," and therefore does not need to consider unsettling new knowledge. When we face newly presented facts about child development in this frame of mind, we can only reject them.

Is it possible to overcome these tendencies in ourselves and to make learning about child development more productive? There is a way, but it is hard, its pace is slow, and its extent depends on the individual makeup of the learner's personality. It consists of using the Socratic method of thinking through and formulating what we know within ourselves, and then adding new facts selectively, at times when we have pinpointed gaps in our knowledge and seek more information. As we contrast old and new facts and ideas, we may decide to revise some old knowledge, or we may find some of the new ideas unacceptable but can at least consider them thoughtfully. An active learning process gets under way. With the help of the newly marshaled and more clearly understood old knowledge we sample and test the new knowledge. Some of it is gradually and effectively linked and interwoven with what we already know, some is set aside, perhaps to remain unacceptable, perhaps to be mastered and integrated later. Sometimes this process of learning proceeds so smoothly and quietly that we hardly know we are learning at all. ("Why, I knew this all along.") Sometimes it leads to joyful moments of insight: "Ah, of course, so that's what it is!" And at other times it frustrates and angers us as we grapple with an unfamiliar idea, doubting or attacking it. The process does not end when the lesson ends, or even when the course ends. We keep mulling things over and reexamining them in the light of later experiences. The idea has become our own thing.

We have found this way of learning child development to be the most successful, although it is time consuming, arduous for both student and teacher, and not without some limitations. Several of us at the Cleveland Center for Research in Child Development have used this method since the early fifties with hundreds of professionals in the fields of health and education as well as with parents. Since 1976 it has been used with many more hundreds of senior high school students. However, all this work of teaching and learning, first without and later with the help of this book and its companion volumes (E. Furman, 1998a, 1998b), has involved personal contact between teachers and students, has utilized lively discussions between them, and has been facilitated by their close working relationship, as described in the *Teacher's Guide* (E. Furman, 1987b).

Can a writer and reader work together in a similar fashion? I trust we can. This volume tries to approximate the same way of teaching, to reach out to you, the interested reader, and to engage your active participation. Your task is not an easy one. It is indeed much more difficult than that of the learner in the classroom. How you go about it and to what extent you use the material is up to you. My good wishes accompany you in your endeavor, and I offer a few suggestions: Before you begin to read a chapter, take time to think about the topic yourself. What do you think and feel about it? Can you relate your ideas to specific situations you have observed or experienced? Do these situations confirm your opinions or are they at odds with them in some instances? What might be the reasons? Perhaps you can figure them out and resolve any discrepancies to your own satisfaction. Perhaps you have even increased your understanding and, like one of my past students, can say, "When you are first asked to figure out your own answers you sort of feel you can't do that and you don't know what to think or say. But once you give it a go, it's really so easy and it all comes so naturally, like finding the pieces of a puzzle and suddenly it all fits. It's fun." Perhaps your puzzle pieces did not fit together and you are left annoyed, with bits and pieces of ideas that don't match. In either case, your efforts will pay off. They may help you to consider and evaluate the written text. Maybe its thoughts and examples will fit in with what you know, maybe they will look at the topic from a different angle, maybe they will seem strange and offer no solutions. Before you decide to accept or reject them, test them out. Observe closely children you know in your work or home, and children you don't know but encounter by chance in the street, supermarket, bus, at the movies, wherever. See whether your observations shed more light on the topic. If you feel sufficiently comfortable with some of the approaches described in the book, try them out and see how they work. You may not feel happy with your effort or with the results, but you will at least gain more food for thought.

When you have worked through a topic, ask yourself what you remember of it, how it related to your experiences with children, what seemed important to you, and what else you would like to know about it.

Regardless of whether you could use all, some, or none of what the book offered, your own mental work will have helped you to see the issues more clearly, to marshal your own thinking and experience, and to pinpoint areas of uncertainty. Perhaps the discussion of the next or later topics will prove helpful, when themes reappear in new contexts or when new ideas illuminate previously presented ones. Your own thinking, like the chapters, weaves to and fro and makes connections. Although the various aspects of child development are arranged in a sequence which facilitates learning, do not hesitate to skip around, to read later chapters, or parts of chapters, first. You may, in this way, want to link an earlier topic with a later one, or you may just be interested in another aspect. In class discussions topics are often interwoven and aspects are taken up "out of order," in keeping with the students' observations, questions, and thoughts. It is your book; use it in the way which you feel best suits your interests. And don't forget that there are two more volumes—*Self-Control and Mastery in Early Childhood* (E. Furman, 1998b) and *Needs, Urges, and Feelings in Early Childhood* (E. Furman, 1998a). Both may help you to tie up loose ends, to get a feel for personality growth as a coherent whole.

Obviously, these books are not intended to impose on you or to convince you. They are neither a big meal you should swallow whole, nor authoritarian dicta you should bow to and believe. Understanding how children develop and mature is a lifelong quest to get to know and appreciate our fellow humans and a part of ourselves. Let us proceed with respect and good will.

1
Different Kinds of Relationships

If someone were to ask us about our experiences with children, we would be likely to think of the different capacities in which we interacted with children, as a baby-sitter, nursery school teacher, children's librarian, camp counselor, tutor, grade school teacher, pediatrician, pediatric nurse. We may have worked in a day care center, played with children in the neighborhood, had younger brothers, sisters, nieces, or nephews; we may be a mother or father. We may think that these experiences taught us a lot, or a little, about a particular child, about children in general, about children in a certain age group. We may feel that our experiences were enjoyable or frustrating, that we did a good job and handled our charges well, or that we failed. And we may think of the children as good or bad, smart or foolish, obedient or obstreperous. And if we were asked what kind of relationship we had with a child, we are apt to describe it as good or bad; good if we liked the child and he seemed to like us and conformed to our demands, and bad if we didn't get along, got angry at one another, and couldn't get him to do as we wished. We rarely think of our relationships with children in terms of different types of relationships with specific functions and goals.

In the adult world we are implicitly aware of these differences. We distinguish a boyfriend–girlfriend relationship, a husband–wife relationship, a friendship, a teacher–student relationship, a doctor–patient relationship, a relationship among co-workers or one between employer and employee, a relationship with neighbors, relationships with different relatives, and many more. Sometimes we welcome it when our tie with a person encompasses two or more types of relationship, such as when a neighbor also becomes a friend. At other times we resent it when our partner in a particular relationship attempts to change its nature, such as when a neighbor starts to act like he or she were our parent, doctor, or lover. Although we expect some relationships to remain the same, with others we take it for granted that they will change. Our relationships with our parents, children, even husband or wife are bound to change to meet the partners' different needs in different phases of life or under special circumstances, such as during periods of illness or special stress. We consider these relationships especially solid and adequate when they can adapt in this way such as when a couple can grow old together, or when one of them can nurse and "mother" the other through a long sickness. We also know how hard such a change can be and how often relationships fail because we cannot accept or bring about a change in their functions and goals such as when parents cannot accept their children's growing up and continue to treat them as dependents.

We usually maintain many different relationships. In each of them our partner shares our understanding of it and joins us in its fulfillment by contributing his or her part. What exactly his or her part is depends of course on the type of relationship, and sometimes on what the partners mutually agree upon, or on the custom of the society they live in. Whereas husband–wife relationships exist all over the world, there are considerable cultural and individual differences in what marital partners expect from their relationship, what each needs to contribute toward its maintenance, and to what extent their contributions are the same or different and complement one another. The relationship is satisfactory to the extent that both parties participate in achieving shared expectations.

In our relationships with children we often do not think along similar lines. We may not be so clear about the nature and functions of our own role with a child; for example, when we baby-sit we may relate to the child as a peer–playmate, but we may fail to think of ourselves as parent-substitutes. We may play or watch TV with them, but may not remind them to keep safety rules or take charge of their getting to bed on time. We usually are even less clear about the child's understanding of his relationship with us; for example, we may not wonder, or try to find out, whether the five-year-old who comes to our activity class expects us to act like his teacher, or baby-sitter, or parent, and even if he does expect us to be his teacher, does he already understand what a teacher–pupil relationship is all about? Does he perhaps just expect us to teach him but not to engage in learning himself? Does he know that a "good" relationship with a teacher shows in a lot of working and learning? When we are confused about our own role, we are apt to confuse the child. When he misunderstands what kind of relationship is appropriate, it will show in inappropriate expectations and behavior. How irritated, frustrated, and unhappy we get with one another when we expect a child to learn what we teach, but he expects us to care for him and demands that we give him candies instead of lessons, or that we accompany him to the bathroom! Yet it does not mean that we are bad teachers or that he is spoiled or naughty. It simply means that there was a misunderstanding about the kind of relationship each expected to develop.

There is, of course, a good reason why we tend to mix our relationships with children and why they so often misunderstand or fail to contribute their part to the kind of relationship we have in mind in a given situation. Children do not necessarily know what different kinds of relationships are about or how they need to participate in them.

What kind of relationship do children know? When do they get to know the other relationships? How do they develop them?

Some people assume that children know only one kind of relationship, namely, that of being taken care of and of having their needs and wants gratified. The child's only contribution to that relationship is to make his demands known and to feel satisfied when they are met. When we attempt to relate to children in this way, we try to gain their love by giving them what we think they want or by allowing them to do as they wish, and we expect them to dislike us when we cross them, let them wait, or make demands on them. We may even feel that we do not matter to them as people in our own right, that they would like anybody who gratifies them, and, when they become dissatisfied, would turn away and seek out another person who would be "nicer" to them in their terms. Although many of us know that such an attitude is a bit exaggerated, that there is more to a child's love than getting what he wants, there is a kernel of truth in this assumption about children's relationships. Children, and young children especially, are indeed very helpless, needy, and dependent, and their survival and well-being hinges on adequate care by others. The primitive bond between the caring, need-fulfilling person and the cared-for, needy one is very basic. It is one part of the parent–child relationship, but it is not the whole story.

We all know that even very young children are not simply satisfied when their needs are fulfilled. When a mother hands over to us the care of her ten-month-old baby, we often find that he does not let us feed him and put him to sleep peacefully. On the contrary, he may altogether forego having his needs gratified by a stranger and may scream or fuss until his mother returns. It seems his mother is more important to him than his food or sleep! A year or so later, when this baby has grown into a toddler, we may meet him and his mother at the grocery store. Instead of sitting contentedly in the seat of the shopping cart and munching his cookies, he is bent on grabbing items off the shelves, poking and tearing packages, demanding to hold things that are apt to spill, and running off into the far aisle. Nor is he necessarily unhappy. The glint in his eyes, the excited screech as he speeds up to escape his mom's pursuit, as well as his skill in finding just those things to do which are contrary to mother's wishes, suggest that he is out for a good fight and tease—his way of having time with Mom. But in another year or so he will be a preschooler and enjoy very different relationships. In his nursery school he will like his teacher, may even like to play cooperatively with other boys and girls, and will be happy to meet his old neighbor who lets him help in the garden. With his mom and dad as well as in all these other new relationships, he will spend much time and effort on showing off and impressing those he loves: "Look at me!"; "See what I can do!" Nothing will please him more than to be admired by them: "My, how strong you are!"; "How big you are!"; "You really look handsome in your new suit." In fact, having a relationship at that age seems to mean the equivalent of a mutual admiration society.

By the time the child gets old enough to be in public school his relationships have changed again. He is ready for a working relationship with his teacher, is eager to learn to read and do arithmetic, shares his teacher with twenty peers, and easily waits several hours for his mother and for his lunch. In the afternoon he may want to play with a friend. On Sunday he enjoys cleaning the car with his dad. He may even join an athletic group and meet with peers and coach in a weekly swim or baseball game. Obviously, this young schoolboy has come a long way and already maintains many different kinds of relationships. Even his relationship with his mother has changed once again. He may like to talk things over with her. He may help her with chores and may make her a present for her birthday. No doubt he still needs and wants her to cook and care for him, but is that not also true of us grown-ups? Don't we look for a measure of need satisfaction in our relationships: a wife who prepares a good meal, a husband who provides money for our wants, a boss who offers pleasant working conditions, a secretary who brings us a cup of coffee?

When we look at relationships in this way we may say that some of the most primitive, early aspects of relationships, those of need satisfaction, diminish in degree as we grow but are never altogether given up. At the same time, the more advanced aspects of relationships—our emotional investment in the other person as a person, rather than as a fulfiller of needs, and our ability to maintain different kinds of relationships with different persons—start quite early and develop gradually during childhood.

When we live with a baby from the time he is born and have a chance to follow his developing relationships day in, day out, until he grows up, we see changes almost every day. We see how new ways of relating make their occasional little beginnings, gradually become more frequent, and eventually overtake an earlier kind of relationship, much as a big wave rolls in over the top of its forerunner. But we also see earlier types of relating resurface at times. Some forward-moving changes come so fast and strong, we can hardly keep up with observing them. At other times there appears to be a lull or return to older patterns. Each child's development has its own unique intricate interplay of forward-running waves and backwash. In addition to their personal ways of developing relationships, all children share an overall progressive sequence of maturational waves. Since the characteristics of each of these waves is most pronounced when it reaches its crest, we often describe them in that form. For the sake of simplicity, we then set aside the many individual variations and focus on what is most typical and what all have in common.

As children's relationships reach one maturational crest after another, they undergo great changes. The differences between successive phases are sometimes much bigger than we realize. For this reason, we can never speak of children as one group of people. At best we can view and compare children at several points in their growth—as babies, toddlers, nursery schoolers, schoolchildren, as preadolescents and adolescents, keeping in mind also that all babies are not alike, all toddlers are not alike, and so on. Each is a unique individual, each encounters different experiences in life, and each copes with them in his or her own way.

We can now begin to answer some of our earlier questions. What kind of relationship do children know? At each stepping stone in their mental growth, children know and maintain the kind of relationship that belongs to that step or phase. Children gradually get to know about different kinds of relationships with different people day by day, year by year, phase by phase. While each child develops in his own way at his own pace, all children's relationships share certain phase-appropriate similarities and characteristics.

Let us now think about the last question we posed: How do children develop these different relationships? When we speak of maturation and successive steps shared by all, we imply an inherent potential, an internal timetable and path that indicate when and in which direction we move along. Yet we all know that children's relationships do not grow automatically, nor do they always reach "the end of the line" to maturity. Some schoolchildren are very appropriate in their relationships with teachers, others are "babies" and expect parental care instead of lessons from their teachers. Even some adults may continue infantile, dependent relationships, or may enjoy fighting and teasing their loved ones as little toddlers do, or showing off to them, like preschoolers. Individual experiences during a person's mental growth account for most of these differences and variations. With relationships particularly, it stands to reason that nurture plays a big part, along with nature. After all, relationships are always a two-way street, one person interacting with another and each affecting the other. We will trace in some detail how relationships develop and change. At the start of this venture, let us keep in mind that each step in growth depends on what preceded it. Just as a house cannot have a second floor without a first one, and a tree cannot sprout a crown without a trunk, so more advanced and varied relationships have to rest on the foundation of earlier ones.

What is the earliest relationship? And how does it come about?

2

The First Relationship—
Mother and Baby

When we think of children under five years old, we recognize very quickly that, however much they may like us and others, their most important relationships are with their parents. And when we are with the youngest ones, the babies and toddlers, there is little doubt in our minds that their first and most intimate bond is with their mothers, or mothering persons. We must know something of that relationship, because the words of the spiritual *Sometimes I Feel Like a Motherless Child* touch a chord in most of us. Even as adults, often or rarely, we have times when we long for someone to accept us as we are and to care for us unconditionally, to comfort us, to protect us from turmoil inside ourselves and from dangers outside, to be with us when we are lonely or to share a good time, to know what we need and to provide it, be it a meal, or a hug, or a kind word. It wouldn't do if just anyone tried to give us all this. We want it to be a person we know so well and who knows us so well that we can trust her to know what we want and to do her part just as we want it, a person with empathy and understanding who cares for nothing more than to care for us.

The young child's relationship with his mother indeed includes this kind of fulfillment of bodily and emotional needs, maintenance of security, protection against excessive stimulation from within and harm from without, gratification of wants, and relief from discomforts. Above all, it includes the assurance that all these "services" will be provided consistently and lovingly, in tune with the child's personality and adapted to the

15

situation at hand. To care in a caring way is the hallmark of mothering. The child's first relationship is with the caring person, the one who mothers him. The child knows her, needs her, wants her, and loves her for it.

There is, however, a big difference between adults who longingly recall what this relationship is about and the young child who experiences it. Preschoolers and even toddlers at times welcome and indeed need their mothers' total and unconditional care, but most of the time they relate to their mothers in much more complex ways. Their ideas of loving and being loved include much more give and take, albeit in infantile forms such as admiring and being admired, or teasing and having a mental tug-of-war for power. Instead of enjoying mother's ministrations, they often much prefer to do for themselves— "Let me do it"; "I want to do it all by myself"—and they are quite often opposed to mother's ideas of what is good for them. We see, therefore, that at these developmental phases, the mother–child relationship has already adapted itself to the child's changing needs. The mother's role no longer focuses primarily on basic need fulfillment but now extends to helping the child to care for himself, to keep himself safe, to modify his wants and urges, and become a social member of the family with new skills (E. Furman, 1992b, 1993).

Babyhood is the only time when the relationship with the mother consists almost exclusively of ongoing empathic fulfillment of bodily and emotional needs. For the baby, this kind of relationship is neither a luxury nor an occasional treat, but a basic necessity. It assures his physical and mental survival. These are strong words. Do they mean that a baby could actually die without this kind of relationship? Yes, they mean just that.

Many people recognize that a baby needs to be fed, kept clean and dry, comforted when ill or in pain, perhaps even picked up and held or rocked at times, but they assume that anyone can perform these ministrations. This is not so. Unless the baby's bodily needs are met often enough by the same person in the same satisfying way so that he can get to know her and rely on his pleasurable interactions with her—that is, form a mutual bond, a relationship—the baby tends to become listless, fails to gain weight and develop, withdraws interest from his surroundings, and becomes prone to infections and diseases to which he succumbs by the end of his first year in some instances. Studies have shown that initially healthy babies die in institutions which provide flawless hygiene and balanced, nutritious feeds but offer no opportunity for establishing a relationship with a consistent caring person. This is not due to cruelty or ill-treatment on the part of the personnel, but inevitably stems from nurses working in shifts and having to care for so many babies that they can merely attend to their bodies (Spitz, 1945, 1946). We do not really know why babies do not live and prosper under adequate physical care. Loving, within an ongoing relationship, seems to be a necessary ingredient.

Winnicott (1940) said that there is no such thing as a baby, there is only a mother-and-baby. He meant not only that a baby is totally helpless on his own and would not survive many days without being cared for, but also that it requires mothering in the sense of consistent loving care. This alone makes need fulfillment a reliably pleasurable experience and gratifies the baby's many emotional needs—mother's companionship, her smiling, touching, looking at him, caressing, her voice and her smell, her stimulations, and her calming of him. This need-fulfilling relationship with the mother is essential for the baby's physical survival and for helping him to thrive in bodily terms. It also lays the foundation of his mind and personality. Through this relationship he gets to know and like himself, forming an idea of "I," and he gets to know and love his mother, forming an idea of "you." One hopes that the first relationship with mother will be "good enough"—again Winnicott's words—to assure that the pleasures he experiences with her will make him seek her and want her for her own sake, and will make him love himself so much that he will not want to come to harm. The love of mother as a person, not just as a fulfiller of needs, will pave the way for all of the child's future relationships, within the family and with outsiders, even as an adult, and will enable him to benefit from these relationships. The liking of himself will serve him to protect his own body and to safeguard his sense of well-being, which is so essential to self-preservation in all of us throughout life. The importance of the first mother–child relationship is not limited to the baby's first year. It serves as the corner-stone of later personality growth.

HOW DOES A BABY FORM THIS FIRST RELATIONSHIP WITH HIS MOTHER?

Newborn babies do not know their mothers or themselves, but they are endowed with a potential for relating to people and for developing a personality. The baby utilizes the pleasurable experiences of having his needs fulfilled as a means for estab-lishing a concept of himself, of mother, and of their interaction. Initially the mother is probably indistinguishable from the self; for example, feeling hunger, pain, sucking and swallowing milk, being contained in holding arms, filling up inside, looking into mother's eyes, and feeling satiated all flow together and make up a unit of experience. Repeated over and over it becomes a memory, an image, without any distinction between parts of self and parts of mother. Even many months later we can observe one-year-olds sitting on mother's lap at times and handling her body as though it were their own. Along with such experiences of oneness come others which gradually show the child that parts of the experience are always there, others not; for example, the hunger and sucking are there but the milk, smiling eyes, and holding arms come and go. When the screaming baby calms down on hearing mother's approaching voice or step, it is a sign that he has made a beginning differentiation between self and mother. His own touching of himself and her handling of him when she changes his diaper or gives him a bath alerts him to other parts of his body as well as to mother's separateness because touching oneself and being touched feel very different.

At best a baby's first-year concept of self includes only some parts of his body—the ones he sees and feels most often. It is a primitive, circumscribed bodily self. His concept of his mother is also limited. He does not know all of her body and even less about her as a personality, but he senses her moods very keenly. Above all he knows when he needs her. As soon as he feels a need he looks or calls for her and his gratifica-tion depends on her meeting his need at once, in the "right" way, in the way he expects it because he is used to it. Even we grown-ups sometimes grumble when we have to wait for a meal, when it is served differently from usual, or does not taste the way we like it. For the baby such delays and changes are sheer tragedy because the familiar constitutes his world and without it his world falls apart. If, however, he can trust that mother fulfills his needs consistently and in the right way his interest gradually shifts from his needs to the mother herself. Up to a point she becomes more important than the needs. When the infant has no bodily needs, mother is called for company, for playing little games, for laughing and cooing together. Sometimes babies love this new part of the relationship with mother so much that they don't want to go to sleep. Having mother with them is so much fun they may refuse to be fed or comforted by others because they miss her so much. In the second half of his first year, when a baby screams at mother's leaving, when he resists being fed by a stranger or cries at the mere sight of the sitter, he is not spoiled. Rather, he has made the remarkable developmental step of knowing and loving his mother and of appreciating her importance in his life. It also implies that he has some idea of himself as separate from her.

The same pleasurable experiences which have enabled the baby to love his mother have also led to his liking his self. It feels good and he wants it to remain feeling good. He protests when he is hurt or uncomfortable or when he is in danger of losing mother, because she is essential to his sense of well-being. The baby who bangs the high chair, throws his toy, screams, or even bites mother's arm in angry protest is not naughty. By directing his "attacks" against mother and things, he shows that he has made the important developmental step of caring for himself and his well-being, and therefore directing his anger away from his own body. In addition to the physiological pain barrier, this loving investment of one's own body is crucial to self-preservation.

AND WHAT ABOUT THE MOTHER'S PART IN THIS RELATIONSHIP?

Under normal conditions, nature assures that the biological mother becomes her baby's consistent caring person, that she has the stamina to perform this arduous task, and derives satisfaction from it. During the many months while the baby lives inside his mother he is a part of herself, bodily and mentally. She knows him as a real separate person only from his movements and hiccups, and her hope or fears about him represent her own thoughts. Birth brings about a big step in perceiving the child as a person in his own right but, at the same time, he remains a part of the mother mentally, and when she holds her baby and nurses him their bodily unit is also restored. The only difference is that before birth the baby was an inside part of her, whereas after birth he is an outside part of her. This feeling of physical and emotional oneness is essential to the mother's own well-being and helps her in her mothering. In caring for him she cares for a part of herself. When she nurses her baby (let's remember that bottle feeding has become possible only very recently), she knows from the sensations in her breasts when the baby gets hungry. Usually her body even awakens her during the night at times when the baby is ready for a feed. The child's satiation coincides with her own relief and makes both of them feel relaxed and comfortable. Nursing becomes a joint pleasurable experience and assures the baby of mother's consistent closeness and care. And when some ill befalls her baby, the mother feels it much as though it had happened to herself. Her own well-being is restored only as he is helped to feel safe and well again. The biblical story of Solomon's judgment reminds us that this special mother–child bond has been recognized and understood through the ages.

Of course, getting to know a new baby, learning to recognize his different cries and signals, and looking after him round the clock is a very demanding job. Even the most devoted, healthy mothers get very tired and do not relish their mothering task all the time. But usually nature gives a mother enough strength and resilience to take full care of her baby, to extend herself to her other children as well, to keep house after a fashion, and even to function a bit as a wife.

However, being the biological mother is not a guarantee of good and enjoyable mothering. A host of factors may interfere with a mother's ability to care for her child effectively, and she may find it difficult or impossible to utilize her natural advantages. Among these factors are ill-health in mother or baby, variations in the mother's psychological makeup, unhelpful advice or lack of support from relatives, doctors, or nurses, or external circumstances, such as financial concerns and worries about her other relationships. The capacity to mother is fostered by natural factors but it is not "instinctive." Some of it stems from a mother's own experiences of being mothered and of developing values of mothering from early models. Other aspects are closely linked to the many specific circumstances of the pregnancy, delivery, postnatal interactions with the baby, and concurrent experiences. Much of mothering has to be learned by being with the baby. In fact, a mother's care of her baby enables her to develop as a mother. If she is separated from her child or has little caring contact with him, maternal development is jeopardized, just as muscles atrophy when they are not sufficiently exercised.

DOES THE CARING PERSON HAVE TO BE THE MOTHER?

In theory anyone can be a good "mother," now that bottle feeding is possible, but the task is immeasurably harder than that of the natural mother. This becomes sadly evident when a mother dies or is permanently separated from her baby, and his care has to be assumed by others. Professional twenty-four-hour nursing care is not only extraordinarily expensive but impossible to arrange with one person, however kind he or she may be. A nurse or housekeeper works at most for ten to twelve hours daily and needs an occasional day off. As a result, two or more nurses need to be employed. Even family members— father, older siblings, or relatives—usually find the total continuous care of the baby too exhausting and need time off to rest, to attend to their other responsibilities and interests, and to take care of their own needs (Barnes, 1964). For them, as it is for the employed nurse, the ongoing, unremitting attention to the baby's needs represents much more giving than getting because they care for the baby as a separate loved one, not as a part of themselves. The baby's satisfaction does not coincide with their own as is true for the functioning natural mother much of the time.

Many adoptive mothers (Schechter, 1970; Menning, 1977; Blum, 1983), some grandmothers, nannies, foster mothers, and some fathers (Pruett, 1983) manage to overcome this handicap. Although the baby never was a part of their own body and cannot return to bodily oneness with them through breast-feeding, their strong wish to mother, as well as their willingness to work at it, may enable them, in time, to form a unit with the baby. Then they not only love him as a separate person but as a part of themselves. It is a remarkable and admirable human achievement.

Fortunately, situations of total substitute care do not arise as often as those of partial or temporary substitute care.

TO WHAT EXTENT IS IT POSSIBLE FOR ONE OR MORE PEOPLE TO SHARE THE CARE OF THE BABY WITH THE MOTHER?

This question may arise from necessity, such as the mother's illness or her need to work to support her family. It may be posed for reasons of convenience or preference: for example, the mother's wish to rest more or devote herself to other interests. Some women's personalities allow them to mother effectively part-time, but if they have to spend all their time with their babies they experience difficulty. For them, part-time substitutes help to preserve the positive aspects of their mothering. The question of substitute care may, however, also be based on the belief that it is helpful to the baby to have more than one person care for him. Some people think that the mother's exclusive care makes a baby too dependent on her and that this accounts for his difficulty in accepting baby-sitters and tolerating separations. Some feel that the more sitters a baby has, the easier it is for him to accept changes. There are others who think that a baby needs more than one relationship and should not be deprived of enjoying other members of the family, acquaintances, or playmates. Some hold that the father in particular should have an equal share in the baby's care so that he will form a relationship with the child and not feel left out. And others yet claim that a mother's absorption with her baby is a cultural phenomenon that stems from the loss of the extended family and results in tying women to the home and depriving them of a full personal life.

Let us consider these concerns.

Many mothers would very much like to devote themselves fully to their babies' care. They suffer and miss their babies when they have to leave them for a part of the day. They fear that their babies suffer from their absence, and they feel bad about their inability to change the circumstances. Some mothers are not forced to go to work but still feel bad when they leave their babies for a few hours occasionally or regularly (L. Furman, 1992, 1993).

It helps to remind ourselves that babies do not need perfect mothering. They need good enough mothering. The important question is whether the mother's care enables her baby to establish and maintain a relationship with her. This does not depend solely on how much time she gives him, but on how she cares for the baby when she is with him, whether she keeps her child in mind even when she is not with him, and how she helps him to tolerate the periods without her. For example, such matters as what kind of sitter she chooses, how she instructs the sitter, how she arranges the transition of care to the sitter, whether the sitter is always the same person, whether the baby remains in familiar surroundings, are all significant. What constitutes good enough mothering depends on the combination of such factors as well as on the nature of the baby. Babies vary in their ability to utilize mothering. Their individual requirements also differ, and change from time to time, such as during periods of illness.

A mother can gauge by the child's physical and mental development whether her plan is working out well. It is a good sign when, toward the middle of his first year, the baby has built an adequate attachment to the mothering person, recognizes her, looks for her, and increasingly in the subsequent months, reacts to her leaving and to her absences. The empathic mother recognizes her baby's ways of reacting. It may be crying, restlessness, unusual alertness, refusal to sleep or withdrawal into sleep, distress on mother's return, changes in eating patterns, and many others. This contrasts with the common belief that all is well if "he doesn't mind and doesn't even notice." Such uncaring behavior may mean that the child is not taking the crucial developmental step from prime interest in need fulfillment to interest in the need fulfilling person. This step may fail to take place, may be delayed, or may be only partially achieved when the baby's early needs have not been fulfilled in a good enough manner or when the ministering person has not been consistently enough the same to meet the baby's confident expectation and deserve his loving investment. Multiple caregivers as well as inadequate care during the first year encourage the child to remain focused on his needs in an egocentric manner and, insofar as he considers the person, to care mainly about how he or she serves him rather than who and what kind of individual he or she is.

The baby's dependence on the mother, at this stage, is a healthy development, as is his difficulty in separating from her and his wariness or protest when others take over his care. Valuing and loving a person does indeed bring with it the fear of losing her and the anger and pain of being separated, but it also goes hand in hand with those aspects of relationships which grow from it and which prove important later on in this and many other societies—loyalty, consideration, and a willingness to forego some of one's own gratifications for the sake of the loved ones. Those who welcome a baby's indiscriminate acceptance of anyone who fills his needs foster a similar self-centeredness and lack of loyalty in the adult, as, for example, one who does not care who his spouse is as long as she satisfies his needs, or one who abandons his children when they are not satisfying. Of course, the one-year-old is not a grown-up person. A baby's age-appropriate attachment is only the first step on the long road toward mature relationships. Actually, the baby's relationship with his mother is far from considerate. He is demanding, uncompromising, and does not hesitate to bite his loved one, and even when he puts food in mother's mouth he is not altruistic but merely enjoys doing to her what she has so often done to him. Nevertheless, without a first relationship with the caring person, the baby can never become a caring adult.

The development of this one-to-one relationship is not necessarily jeopardized when a baby is held or handled by a sitter. Family members are often the best sitters. The child is used to seeing them, and they have a special investment in him.

The extended family can indeed be very helpful as long as it is congenial and supportive.*

However, during the first few months, the baby does not appreciate the caregivers as people in their own right. He accepts their care as satisfactory to the extent that it approximates that of the main mothering person. When their way of meeting the baby's needs differs from hers it upsets him. At this stage, it is important that the baby's upsets not be so frequent and so severe as to interfere with his ability to get to know his mother and himself. He has as yet no capacity or want for varied relationships. He does not miss even his father, unless the father is his main mothering person.

DOES THAT MEAN FATHERS ARE LEFT OUT? WHAT IS THEIR ROLE WITH THE BABY?

A man may wish that he could bear a child and may envy the special biological and psychological bond of the mother–child unit. But the fact that he cannot have this role does not make him redundant nor does he have to content himself with being a mother-substitute. Some fathers like baby-sitting and do it well, others don't. This is not their most important contribution, nor is it the only or even the best avenue toward a relationship with the infant. The father's special role with the baby is altogether different from that of the mother or principal caregiver (R. A. Furman, 1983).

The father–child relationship develops along somewhat different lines from the mother–child relationship. While the

*The frequent lack of an extended family in our society has led to some misconceptions about it. Prior to the perfection of bottle feeding, the mother had to nurse her baby and, as a result, could never leave him for long, regardless how many others were ready to take over. In preindustrial societies, where nursing on demand is customary and complementary foods are unavailable, the mother usually carries her child with her for many months wherever she goes and while she works. Also, while the extended family is always available, a mother cannot choose to accept or reject it. The closer the ties are with the extended family group, the more a society tends to regulate the role of each member and the ways in which they interact. The individual usually has little or no freedom of choice. Thus, for different reasons and in different ways, a mother's complaint about being tied down and not being able to realize her own personal potential during her child's babyhood has been as applicable in the past and in other culture patterns as in our present society.

baby is never an integral part of his body, mentally and emotionally, however, the infant is very much a part of him, and in this respect his earliest, even prenatal, relationship with the baby parallels the mother–child relationship. During the baby's first weeks and months, the father's role and gratification does not lie in his direct interaction with the baby but in his ability to relate to the mother–child unit as a whole. This enables him to feel with mother and baby, to protect and support them, and to be active on their behalf vis-à-vis the environment at the time of their greatest vulnerability. In this way the father's role in relation to the mother–child unit is akin to the mother's role with the infant: in caring for them he cares for himself. When the father is prevented from assuming this part, because of external circumstances or for reasons within his own personality, his development as a father is jeopardized, as happens with the mother when she is deprived of contact with her baby. But, beyond that, the father's special investment of the mother–child unit is essential to the mother who builds her relationship of devotion to the child with the help of his devotion to them. In this complex and mutually dependent interaction, each represents to the other both a loved person and a part of his or her self. This double investment, though different in mother and father, makes the parent–child relationship unique. In the first year, the mother functions as a part of the child and helps him build his initial self. In addition to his role of protecting and supporting the mother–child unit, the father, and others who are close to the infant, soon begin to meet the baby's developing interest in relationships with people other than the mothering person. At later points in the child's growth the father's role changes and both parents complement aspects of their son's or daughter's personality.

WHEN IS A BABY READY FOR ADDITIONAL RELATIONSHIPS?

When the baby's needs are no longer as urgent as they were initially, and when his relationship with his mother has progressed to the point where he loves her as a person, the infant begins to show interest in other people and derives pleasure and stimulation from their different human responses. As long as he feels assured of mother's presence and available care, the well-developed baby in the latter part of his first year welcomes familiar people's specific approaches. He enjoys special brief interactions with them and builds individual relationships unrelated to need fulfillment with the father, with older siblings, and with other familiar people. One boy had lost his father through death at eleven months of age. For many years he kept poignant memories of little games with his dad and of the special way his dad picked him up high for a hello hug. In this kind of early relationship the father is loved as a person in his own right. The perception of him—his different look, feel, sound, and smell—is appreciated and the interaction he offers enriches the little child's experiences.

Of course, this specific early father–child relationship exists only in addition to the need-fulfilling mother–child relationship. When a need arises in mother's presence, such as fatigue or a hurt, the baby usually quickly abandons his father, and cries and reaches for his mother. When a need arises during mother's absence, the baby treats the father as a mother-substitute who pleases the child when he acts as much as possible like the mother. The additional new relationships seem brief but they are important developmental steps.

WHAT HAPPENS WHEN THE EARLY MOTHER–BABY RELATIONSHIP IS NOT SO IDEAL, WHEN STRESSES INTERFERE?

For many of us and for many who are close to us, life has indeed been far from ideal. When we think about the importance of the early mother–child relationship we often wonder how we, and those we know, weathered the hardship of early upheavals and what impact they have had on later development. Let us look at some of the interferences, gauge their effect on the baby, and consider different ways in which they may be dealt with.

WHAT HAPPENS WHEN EARLY MOTHERING IS INADEQUATE, SUCH AS WHEN A MOTHER DOES NOT REALLY WANT HER BABY?

In the light of what we said earlier, a totally unwanted and uncared for child does not survive. The adequacy and inadequacy of mothering is difficult to rate on a scale. It has to be gauged by the baby's responses and development. If his care was poor, by average standards, but the infant is in fair physical and emotional health, he must have received a measure of loving care that was good enough. The infant probably managed to utilize its positives to best advantage. Sometimes a mother comes to love a child she was not ready for earlier and is then able to help her child catch up or make up. To some extent, and within certain individual time limits, infants can utilize a later opportunity, compensate for what they had missed, or modify earlier experiences (Provence and Lipton, 1962).

WHAT HAPPENS WHEN EARLY MOTHERING IS INTERRUPTED TEMPORARILY THROUGH SEPARATION, OR PERMANENTLY, SUCH AS WHEN THE MOTHER DIES OR WHEN THE BABY IS TAKEN FROM A FOSTER HOME AND PLACED IN AN ADOPTIVE HOME?

When an infant has to cope with a separation or a complete change of mothering person, he undergoes a major stress. However, it is always better to have had some good mothering and lost it than never to have had it at all. Built-up reserves from good care and his own stamina may enable him to cope with the upheaval and, in time, to continue his development. The effects of separations and of changes in mothering person also depend very much on the timing and circumstances. For example, a gradual takeover of care by a familiar person who is able to recognize and soothe the child's upset reaction, differs greatly from a sudden shift to a stranger who is unable to understand and meet the baby's needs.

The younger the baby, the more his upset tends to show in bodily distress. The older baby's feeding and sleep patterns may also be interfered with for some time but he is likely to have an additional, more specific emotional response to the loss of the loved person. He may show fear, sadness, and anger. These are appropriate signs that he is acknowledging the difficult reality and attempting to master the situation. Indications of more severe distress are loss of appetite, loss of weight, physical ill-health, or prolonged periods of bodily discomfort, loss of interest in the surroundings, withdrawal, listlessness, apathy.

Although separations and changes in mothering person are indeed stressful events for a baby, he often manages to overcome them and to continue to develop with the help of his own strength and the loving care extended to him.

WHAT, IF ANY, ARE THE LASTING DAMAGES OF INADEQUACIES, INTERRUPTIONS, OR CHANGES IN MOTHERING?

Most people's early upsets and stresses, just like their good experiences, play a part in shaping their personalities and contribute to their individuality and uniqueness. Each has his quirks and idiosyncrasies, each also has his weak spots which may not bother him much or which, like old scars, may be touched off only now and then under special circumstances when current experiences combine with old trouble spots. Early hurts and deficits are sometimes overshadowed by later development and compensated for with the help of subsequent achievements.

However, not all of us are so fortunate. In some cases early upheavals and deficits combine with stresses during the toddler and preschool stages; in others the unhappy experiences during babyhood actually impair the infant's development and leave lasting scars. Of these the most serious are an infant's inability to build or renew his beginning relationship with a loved one and to establish or reconstitute a sense of bodily well-being.

If a baby was never able to make the step from wanting need-fulfillment to relating to the need-fulfilling person for her own sake, or if the interruptions of such a relationship produced such a setback that the baby could not rebuild this kind of relationship, all his future capacity for relationships may be jeopardized. This not only deprives him of the pleasure of later relationships but also interferes with his personality development because it is formed with the help of later relationships. Studies have shown that inadequately formed and/or repeatedly interrupted relationships during the early years may result in psychopathic, criminal, and some forms of delinquent personalities (Bowlby, 1944, 1951; Friedlander, 1947; A. Freud, 1949). This may contribute to major difficulties in maintaining adult close relationships and in functioning as a parent.

The second area of difficulty, the poor sense of bodily well-being, may affect a person's later ability to like and safeguard his body. This may contribute to bodily ills stemming from psychological causes, to accident proneness, or to suicidal tendencies. Whereas personality difficulties that result from later developmental interferences usually can be treated and helped, those aspects that are rooted in the earliest deficits tend to be unalterable (Fleming, 1974).

IS IT ALWAYS THE FAULT OF MOTHERING WHEN CHILDREN HAVE DIFFICULTIES?

The role of parenting is so important that all of a child's ills are often attributed to parental failure, but it is not always the mother's fault. Parents themselves feel so responsible for their children's development and welfare that they tend to accept the blame. Even in babyhood, however, when mothering is indeed of supreme importance, it is not the only important factor.

A baby's individual endowment and physical health play a crucial part. For example, an infant's congenital deficit, such as blindness, deafness, or a neurological problem, may interfere with his capacity to get to know and distinguish mother and self; or an anomaly of his mouth or digestive tract may render eating consistently unpleasurable; or an illness and necessary medical and surgical treatments may impose their own severe stresses. Hospitalization may, in addition, cause interruptions in mothering. There are also subtler difficulties in babies which may make them more vulnerable and less able to utilize mothering; for example, a very low tolerance for stimuli from within and without may cause ordinary noises or minor changes in routine to be experienced as very distressing and disruptive. To some extent, mothers can adapt themselves to the special needs of each child and their particularly empathic care may even compensate for the stresses caused by other factors. However, in some situations even the best mothering cannot provide a continuous and pleasurable enough milieu to foster the early developments.

The older the child, the more structured his own personality becomes, and the more he interacts with the wider community, the less can we look to mothering as the sole or primary cause of the child's difficulties. Even with careful and skilled professional investigation, it is sometimes hard to determine the part played by past or present mothering and the way it interacts with other old and recent experiences to produce specific psychological problems.

DOES IT MAKE A DIFFERENCE WHETHER A BABY IS NURSED OR BOTTLE-FED?

When a mother wants to nurse her baby, works at establishing breast-feeding (it usually takes a few weeks to accomplish), and comes to enjoy it, it is the easiest and most satisfying way for the mother to feed her baby and affords both of them a natural opportunity to be close and to get to know and love each other. However, when a mother is not comfortable with the idea of nursing, or when she is unable to breast-feed, she can use the bottle-feeding periods similarly as a way of relating with the baby. The important factor is that feeding be accompanied by loving care and personal interaction. Unfortunately, both nursing and bottle-feeding can be administered impersonally or without being in proper tune with the child's emotional needs (A. Freud, 1946, 1947, 1953; L. Furman, 1992, 1993).

DOES THE CHILD'S ORDER IN THE
FAMILY MAKE A DIFFERENCE TO HOW
HE IS MOTHERED?

Each child receives his own kind of mothering. With each child the mother has to invest herself anew and build a unique mother–child relationship. Its special nature does not depend on the numerical order of the child within the family but on other factors—the baby's looks and responses, the mother's physical and emotional health, the experiences associated with the child's birth, and other current and past circumstances. The mother's previous experiences with mothering will also play a part. They may prove helpful or make it more difficult.

IS EARLY MOTHERING DIFFERENT
FOR TWINS?

Each twin requires individual good enough mothering. His twinship is not a substitute for maternal care; on the contrary, it is more likely to be a measure of interference. The twins' simultaneous needs may make it harder for a mother to attend adequately to both children, especially if their smallness at birth requires more frequent feedings and special handling. Also, twins may be an additional source of unhelpful stimulation to one another; for example, a twin may be awakened by the other's cry or by the noises that accompany the other's care. Some admirable mothers manage nevertheless to give each twin good enough individual mothering.

WHAT ABOUT CULTURAL DIFFERENCES
IN EARLY MOTHERING?

There are many individual and cultural variations in mothering. However, all need to provide good enough continuous loving care to assure a baby's physical survival and to lay the foundation for his mental development—a beginning concept of self and of the person(s) he seeks to fulfill his bodily and emotional needs. The extent to which these needs are satisfied or frustrated and the manner in which it is done affect the ways in which the child's personality develops. And this is where individual, cultural, and racial differences in child rearing begin, in that they determine to a considerable extent the mothering person's choice of which needs she will gratify, when and how. For example, a mother's handling of the baby's sucking (breast, bottle, or own thumb) and his eating (self- or spoon-feeding, soft or chewy foods) shapes not only his attitudes to feeding but many developing character qualities—dependence or independence, tendency to seek and enjoy new pleasures or to persist with the familiar, ability to substitute one gratification for another, or insistence on a certain form of satisfaction. At the time it may seem of little consequence whether he nurses a few more months or sucks his fingers or holds his bottle before sleeping, or whether, when, and how he gets to like new foods. However, in their own way, and little by little, these early variations in mother–child interaction become the building blocks of the child's personality with its own characteristics and values, and make him suited to adjust within his own family and community.

3
The Baby-sitter

Baby-sitting is often regarded as an unskilled and unimportant job, and perhaps for that reason most of us have had some experience with it, at one time or another. If all seemed to go well, we considered ourselves good sitters. If, as happens more often, things did not go so well, we may have blamed the child's parents, or they may have blamed us, or, most likely, parents and sitter reproached the child for being naughty. Actually, baby-sitting, like parenting, is a difficult, skilled, and important job. The sitter takes the parent's place and is entrusted with the child's safety and welfare, at least temporarily and to some extent. Being responsible for someone's life and well-being is no minor task, especially when that somebody is unable to take care of himself.

As adults we are so used to functioning independently that it is difficult to empathize with the young child's predicament, except perhaps when we become very ill. Then we may find ourselves nearly as helpless and incompetent, and as dependent on others to make us safe and comfortable. In that situation most of us want to make quite sure that we can really trust our caregivers—doctor and nurse—to do right by us. We don't like it at all when "our" doctor or nurse leaves us in the care of substitutes we don't know so well or who may not know enough about us. We certainly would get very upset if we found that our physician, or his substitute, did not take the job of looking after us very seriously. Our feelings would become the more intense and urgent, the more we would be incapacitated and unable to care for our own needs. And imagine if, on top of all that, we could not talk and make ourselves understood! Just like a baby!

Baby-sitting, however, is not only important to our little charges. It is also important to us as sitters. Our role as parent-substitutes brings us into close contact with the most intimate parts of children's lives and affords us a unique opportunity to observe, study, and understand them. Let us therefore look closer and trace the course of the infant's dependence on need fulfillment and how this affects his developing relationships.

BABY-SITTING WITH BABIES

We know already that the consistent loving care by the mothering person paves the way for the baby to experience a sense of well-being and to get to know himself and the person he depends on for his comfort. As soon as the mother and her way of taking care are sufficiently remembered to feel familiar and to be expected (and this can happen within a few weeks or a couple of months), the baby also recognizes changes in person and care and reacts to them with varying degrees of distress, usually accompanied by behavioral changes. The baby-sitter may find it difficult to feed the baby, or to comfort his crying, or to calm him enough to help him go to sleep.

Within a few more months the infant comes to appreciate his mother as being so essential to his bodily and mental welfare that he may not feel safe unless he is fully assured of her availability. He may not even want to be held by a stranger when he can see mother, much less when she is not around. He has no way to understand that he will survive with the help of others or that mother will eventually return. Her leaving means the end of his world. It is not uncommon for babies to respond with rage and/or inconsolable distress and even to refuse need fulfillment when they are suddenly left with a stranger. And waking up to see a strange face often marks the beginning of weeks of sleep disturbance.

No doubt, some of us have also had the experience of "never having much trouble" with a baby. This usually happens when the baby has had a lot of opportunity to get to know us in his mother's presence, when she has fully acquainted us with her ways of taking care, and has perhaps gradually allowed us to do some things for him under her supervision, and when he has experienced our care only during brief maternal absences. Seeing us with mother then comes to mean something like, "Mom is going away but will come back, and this substitute is pretty okay." The process of getting acquainted and learning to trust the baby-sitter is especially prolonged and laborious during babyhood because there are as yet no words to explain matters and no abstract thinking with which to grasp them. Of course, with baby-sitters who are members of the family there is a built-in way of getting to know them in mother's presence which makes it much easier.

Although their dependence on the loved one is great, babies are not as helpless as it seems. From their third month on, they usually master the skill of sucking their own thumb or fingers and can utilize it to give themselves pleasure and comfort quite independently. It is a remarkable achievement in many ways and differs greatly from the random sucking that takes place in utero and postnatally when the hand happens to be near the mouth but cannot be actively brought to it or kept there. Active thumb sucking helps the baby to differentiate self from nonself, to get to know a new part of his body, to manipulate it at will. Moreover, the thumb is always available, in contrast to mother who may take a while to respond to the child's signals, and in contrast also to a pacifier which falls out and cannot be retrieved by the child himself. Although thumb sucking cannot still big hunger or relieve other really pressing needs, it goes quite a ways in alleviating little discomforts and tensions, both bodily and emotional. When we watch a baby waking up we can witness how a small need grows into a big one and to what extent sucking helps to ease it. We may first observe sucking movements, then active thumb or finger sucking for quite a while, and only eventually crying bursts out. Once babies can suck their thumb or fingers they can take care of some needs on their own, can wait a little for other needs to be met, and can more easily calm and comfort themselves before falling asleep. In short, they have taken a step toward independence. Some mothers, for that very reason, do not welcome thumb sucking. They link it in their minds with all the later ways in which children will want to do their own thing, will not need the parent, and therefore perhaps will be impervious to the parent's injunctions. Yet, in other ways, parents value a child's independence and a baby who sucks his thumb is a good bit easier to take care of, for mother and sitter.

In the latter part of the first year, infants often acquire another way of comforting themselves. This new way helps them particularly to deal with the longing for mother, who is now seen as a separate person and who is not always close by. I am referring to the fact that babies create a *transitional object*. The term was coined by Winnicott (1953), elaborated by Stevenson (1954), and refers to the space between infant and mother, the transition between them. Characteristically, the transitional object is not a part of the child's or mother's body, but something that reminds the child a bit of each or represents a part of their interaction. Out of many possible objects in his environment, the baby chooses a certain one and invests it with a symbolic meaning. It is his first imaginative creation and, in this sense, is the forerunner of his later much more complex and sophisticated creativity. The transitional object may be a piece of soft blanket or its silky lining, a diaper, a soft small toy. There are many individual variations in its shape, texture, smell, or other quality that may feel essential about it to the infant. The baby's choice of materials, like his budding imagination, is limited. Even a pacifier or milk bottle can become a transitional object and may account for the fact that the child is unwilling to relinquish them for many months or even years. Many of us remember our own transitional object, that first treasured possession which mothers often help safeguard, sensing its importance. The transitional object does not make the child as self-sufficient as his own thumb because a "blankie" can fall out of reach or get lost, but it is easier to keep around than mother. Many a baby-sitter has been saved much trouble by the fact that the infant or young toddler could use his blanket or soft toy to ease the stress of being separated from his mother.

The older baby is also beginning to do some things for himself, particularly drinking from a cup and eating solid foods. This too makes him less directly dependent on mother and sitter.

The more "independent" a baby is and the more ways he has of comforting himself, the more he is ready to seek and enjoy the familiar baby-sitter as a person in his own right, not just as a mother-substitute. He may like a specific little hand game or song which the sitter introduces and which becomes an expected pleasurable interaction in their relationship. Games of the peek-a-boo variety often become favorites because their theme of predictable go away–come back, disappearance and reappearance, helps to master the presence and absence of the mother which preoccupies so much of the older baby's feeling and thinking.

BABY-SITTING FOR TODDLERS

We can observe further changes in the interaction between need fulfillment and the mother–child relationship when we baby-sit with toddlers (roughly between the ages of one-and-a-half to two-and-a-half years old).

Sandra, at twenty-two months, often visited her aunt's home with her mother and enjoyed playing with her teenage cousins who joked and frolicked with her and allowed her to play with many of their things to her heart's content. She was usually reluctant to leave, dawdled, and begged to stay on. One day her wish was granted. An overnight visit was planned. Sandra seemed to look forward to it, arrived proudly with her little bag of belongings and hardly bothered to bid her mother goodbye. All went well. Dinner was a bit hectic with Sandra messing and grabbing at foods, running to and from the table, and wetting herself although she usually kept herself clean. This was attributed to her being so busy and having extra fun, rather than as a sign of her missing her mother. It was only at the next period of need fulfillment, bedtime, that Sandra's longing for her mother overwhelmed her. When going to bed could no longer be put off, she began to cry for her mother and was so upset that the mother was called, came and took her home.

Marc, at twenty-three months, had met his baby-sitter several times in mother's presence. On the day when the sitter was to look after him she arrived in the afternoon. Marc had already been told that Mom and Dad would go out for the evening. He followed the grown-ups around, listening on and off to mother telling the sitter about where things were and what their routines were like. After the parents were gone, Marc began to show the sitter around. He introduced her to his toys and books and told or indicated to her what she was to play with him. But he was not keen on doing what she asked of him and he would not allow her to do anything for him. He was intent on doing everything all by himself, even when he was not really up to it. He insisted on climbing into and out of his high chair, pouring his own milk from the pitcher, pulling the cookie box off the shelf, turning on his bathwater, putting on his pajamas (half way and backwards). With some activities, his independence was merely time-consuming, with others it led to messes and near disasters. Regardless, he adamantly refused help, resented interference, and persisted in his efforts while the sitter trailed and hovered near him attempting to keep him safe. When he finally dropped off to sleep, clutching his teddy with one arm and sucking his thumb with the other, the exhausted sitter had to tackle the extensive cleanup in the wake of Marc's independence.

John, aged two years, five months, had his grandparents as sitters for a day and night while his parents went out of town. He knew his grandparents quite well from periodic visits. He also was a clever thinker and talker, could understand his mom's explanation of and preparation for the separation, and could make his own needs known in words. All this helped him to have a rather good though subdued day with his sitters, who entertained him appropriately. He refused to nap, ate a small dinner, and, in the evening, put off getting ready for bed. Although it was getting late and he was obviously tired, there was still always one more thing he wanted to do. His bunny, which had been unattended to during the earlier part of the day, was now being clutched tightly. When grandmother finally insisted on "bathtime now," he protested angrily and then wailed a heartrending, "I want my mommy to wash me." Grandma compromised by washing him with a lick and a promise and allowed him to wash his bunny. This calmed him and he later announced that he had washed both bunny and himself! The next stressful time was lying down to sleep. Angry screams and tears were finally helped by Grandma staying with him for a while, telling him that Mom and Dad loved him and would return in the morning, and by bunny being tucked in with him.

All three children were healthy, well-functioning toddlers. They could walk, understand, and use speech to a considerable extent, and were interested in things and people. Compared to the needy dependent baby, they were quite self-sufficient. They could feed themselves, could get around and help themselves to some foods, could ask for what they wanted in words. They could get most of their clothes off and could help with getting some of them on. At times they could even use the toilet to keep clean and dry.

How did this relative independence affect their relationships? It certainly made for a marked change. The toddlers had much more wish, time, and energy for relationships with people other than the mother and they enjoyed interactions with friendly adults in her presence. Sandra had so much fun with her cousins that she repeatedly wanted to stay with them. It was only when these "additional" relationships assumed the role of mother-substitutes during the mother's absence that the toddlers did not welcome the sitters' ministrations. At the peak times of bodily and emotional need they either preferred to forego need satisfaction (small dinners, refusal to be washed and go to bed), or they wanted to fill their own needs (especially Marc), or they angrily and helplessly called for their mothers. Marc and John could comfort themselves better with the help of thumb sucking and their soft toys. Sandra, who had no means of self-comfort, became overwhelmed.

In the course of development, the need-fulfilling early bond with the mother is not transferred to the relationships with others, except under the stress of necessity or, occasionally, as a way to tease Mom ("Today I want Grandma to tuck me in"). Normally, the early relationship with the mother is used to assist the child in learning to take care of himself. The more and better the child gradually achieves what we might call "being mother to himself," the more are his relationships with parents and others freed of basic need-fulfilling dependency. The parental role of caring for the child goes hand in hand with that of helping him to care for himself. This task begins with caring for one's own bodily needs. It ends in young adulthood when people take care of themselves in the fullest sense of the word, including earning their own living and looking after their health. Many young adults, usually quite independent at college or in their job, still call home when they get sick, before they call a doctor (E. Furman, 1992b, 1993).

All along, the job of self-care, of mothering oneself, includes not only the gratification of needs but some of the giving of love that is part and parcel of the mother's early bodily care. As she encourages and appreciates the child's care of himself she invests that love in the process of her teaching and his learning, and it becomes part of his liking to care for himself. Marc's insistence on doing everything for himself has many reasons. One of them is loving himself as mother would love him if she were there. A child may well enjoy the company of a familiar sitter and trust him to a considerable extent to fill many aspects of the parental role, but it is always more difficult for him to hand over the care of his body. The younger the child and the less he can do for himself, the harder it is to accept the sitter for need fulfillment. However, even much older children want nobody but their mom at times of illness, injury, or danger to their welfare. At these times once again they feel unable to care for their own bodies. This is also true in periods of mental stress, of misfortune, upset, or loneliness, when children and even adults reexperience early feelings of helplessness and distress and long for the mother's loving care for which it is so difficult to substitute.

The children in our examples were neither ill nor threatened by special danger or misfortune. They only suffered the mental stress of separation. Even that was considerably lessened for them by their mothers' explanations and preparation, by their own understanding of when mother would return, and by their relationships with the familiar sitters. The sitter, and even more so, the toddler, would have had a much harder time if the child had not known the sitter, had been surprised by his mother's absence and known nothing about her return, or if the child had become ill or injured. Such distress may have shown at the time in crying, in being very angry, uncooperative, or unapproachable, in reverting to babylike behavior, such as crawling and babbling, or in upsets around eating, toileting, and sleeping. Oftentimes toddlers appear to manage the stressful period well, but the disturbance manifests itself later and may then persist for a long time. Sitters cannot know of such aftermaths and even parents may miss the links between the stress of separation and the subsequent behavioral changes or disturbance. The individual variations of ensuing difficulties are too great to enumerate. Among the more common ones are fears, clinginess, or the opposite, namely, wandering off and getting "lost," interferences in sleeping, eating, and toilet training, and exacerbations of conflicts in the mother–child relationship.

The toddler's relationship with his mother is, in any case, much less harmonious than it was during babyhood. Sandra, Marc, and John showed some of the toddler's typical determination and contrariness, attempt to control the adult, the drive to do everything oneself and go off and explore, especially where one is not supposed to. Although some of their behaviors were exaggerated with the sitter, such as Marc's "me-do-it," others would have been more noticeable with their mothers, such as teasing, provoking, and mixing love and anger to such an extent that it would often be difficult for Mom to tell whether a hug was meant to be a caress or an attack. Some mothers describe this relationship by saying, "My child is so positive these days," and others call it, "so negative." We might say that, whereas the baby uses his mother to learn to recognize her and himself as different bodies, the toddler utilizes his relationship with his mother to establish her and himself as separate minds, and tests the limits of their boundaries. The toddler can better distance himself the more he can count on mother's availability, on her just being there. Wanting to care for himself, learning how to do it, and turning to things and people for new pleasures, all are a part of this healthy maturational step. But mother has to be there to be left and to be returned to at will. When mother is not there physically, or when she is emotionally unavailable for more than a few hours, the toddler's newly gained mental self is endangered and the threat of needs going unfulfilled again becomes paramount. Some toddlers may then react by reverting to extreme dependency; others may adopt a precocious defensive independence and distance themselves from the give and take of relationships, as if to say, "You don't need me, so I don't need you" and perhaps even, "I don't need anybody." The strange sitter has no way to help the child. The familiar and understanding sitter can assist him in mastering a stressful period.

Some people think that baby-sitting for the littlest ones is easy because their needs are so basic and their powers so limited. Actually baby-sitting with them is the most difficult because for them the stress of separation from the mother is so great, and they find it so hard to accept substitutes.

WHAT HAPPENS WHEN THERE IS A SEVERE INTERFERENCE IN THE TODDLER'S RELATIONSHIP WITH HIS MOTHER, SUCH AS LONG OR REPEATED SEPARATIONS, PERMANENT INTERRUPTION, INADEQUATE MOTHERING, ILLNESS, AND HOSPITALIZATION?

In the case of all major stresses during the first year, a great deal depends on how they are handled, who takes the place of the mothering person, and whether several stresses coincide or follow one another in close sequence. The individual child's disposition and stamina also vary as well as the nature of his earlier development and subsequent experiences. The caring adults can always find more helpful ways of assisting a child in coping with stresses when they appreciate that his situation is very difficult. With appropriate help even the most severe upsets can be mastered or at least alleviated (E. Furman, 1984).

Insofar as the toddler–mother relationship helps the child to differentiate his personality from hers, to achieve an appropriate balance between independence and dependence, and to learn to love mother in spite of some conflicts and disappointments, interferences in the mother–child relationship at that stage threaten these developments. This may manifest itself in personality disorders which make a person focus on himself and be unable to relate to or feel with others. In extreme cases it may lead to self-centered, impulse-ridden, psychopathic or delinquent behavior. Another pathology, almost opposite in form, may show in primitive dependence on loved ones, inadequacy in independent functioning, difficulty in being alone, and severe emotional reaction to loss and disappointment. In extreme cases it contributes to some forms of depression or mental prostration.

Among the more common milder consequences are persisting aspects of toddler characteristics in relationships: for example, an excess of mixed feelings, argumentativeness, hostility, possessiveness, and a need to control the loved one (E. Furman, 1981a).

However, severe interferences in the mother–toddler relationship may also affect other areas of the personality and its maturation. For example, the development of speech and its effective use for thinking and communication are linked primarily to the ongoing mother–toddler relationship and to the mother's enjoyment of talking with her child (E. Furman, 1992b, 1993; Hall, 1982).

ARE THUMB SUCKING AND "BLANKET"-TYPE POSSESSIONS REALLY HELPFUL? DO THEY NOT DEVELOP INTO BAD HABITS AND "PROPS" THAT MAKE A CHILD LOOK BABYISH LATER, MAKE HIS TEETH GROW CROOKED, AND ARE UNHYGIENIC?

Many responses and behaviors which are healthy and appropriate at one developmental level may become inappropriate and indicative of difficulty at later stages. Normally, thumb sucking gives way to other forms of self-comfort as the child grows older and transitional objects tend to be replaced by dolls and toys which the child uses for imaginative and manipulative play. By the time he attends nursery school, thumb sucking and transitional objects are used occasionally or not at all. When early behavior persists, it is not because it was there in the first place but because something got in the way of its being replaced by a more advanced form; for example, thumb sucking in later phases may have lost its original function and come to represent the child's attempt at coping with different stresses and conflicts. When a person keeps on wearing the same dress, year in, year out, for all occasions, we would probably not think that this could have been avoided if she had never gotten that dress. We would rather wonder what her reasons are for not changing to a different dress.

BABY-SITTING WITH PRESCHOOLERS

Well-developed three-, four-, and five-year-olds are often most enjoyable to baby-sit with, provided they know and trust the sitter, understand where mother is, and can gauge the time of her return, and provided also that they are neither ill nor under special stress. Need fulfillment and relationships are by then much less intertwined and self and mother are much more clearly and stably conceived as separate persons in the preschooler's mind. Relationships with others are assuming a new importance as well, so that the sitter is not only a mother substitute but a potentially interesting person. With and from the sitter one can learn more about the world and he or she can also supply the ever welcome admiration for the child's "Look at me," "See what I have," and "See what I can do."

Four-year-old Jennifer first met her sitter-to-be on an afternoon outing to the ice cream parlor which her mother had arranged as a pleasant way to get acquainted. Jennifer had a chance to boast of all the things she had and could do and asked many questions of the sitter, including some personal ones about the sitter's clothes, jewelry, home, and family. On the day mother was to leave Jennifer for the evening, they all had several hours together in the home first. Jennifer participated in showing the sitter around and familiarizing her with all the rules and routines. Mother served Jennifer an early dinner. After the parents left there were games and stories and a long period of Jennifer dressing up like a big lady, saying goodbye to her dolls, and tucking them into the doll buggy. She was proudly independent in taking her bath and getting ready for bed and basked in the sun of the sitter's praise and admiration, but she could also ask for and accept help appropriately. Actual bedtime was a little harder. Jennifer's teddy "needed" two extra stories and there was a call for a drink after lights out. When the sitter reminded Jennifer of Mom's bedtime rule, Jennifer said that Mom could not really know because she was not home, so couldn't she stay up later. When this was refused, she asked wistfully whether it was time yet for Mom and Dad to return and then asked the sitter to be sure to remind them to kiss her as soon as they arrived. The sitter promised and Jennifer dropped off to sleep.

Although this is not an unusual baby-sitting experience, we all can no doubt recall others that were nowhere near as smooth. Unfortunately, children at that age often cannot yet tell us—sometimes do not even realize—what concerns them: "I miss my Mom"; "I am mad she left me"; "I am worried she won't come back"; "She likes going out with Dad better than staying home with me"; "She doesn't love me"; "I don't love her, she was mean today"; "I want to be grown up, I want to do what I please"; "I hate having a sitter instead of Mom." Instead of knowing and verbalizing their concerns, children may show them in fears, disobedience, crying over little things, or distracting themselves with excited fun and exaggerated activity, or resenting the sitter and making life miserable for her.

When the stress is minor, children's own means of coping are adequate; for example, Jennifer used dressing up and doll play to cope with her wish to go out like mother and to leave others rather than be left herself. She gained self-esteem from her independent dressing and bathing. She used the sitter for comfort at bedtime, and she asked in words about the parents' return and love for her. Some children can be helped when the sitter speaks with them of the parents, of their and the child's missing of one another, of how hard it can be to feel left out, and of how pleased they will all be to be together again

When the stress is major, the child's means prove inadequate and thoughts and feelings get to be expressed in behavior that is not appropriate. Just how big the stress is depends not only on the actual circumstances of the specific baby-sitting period but includes all the many factors which have affected the child's life recently and in the past. When the stress becomes excessive, the young child's personality achievements crumble. Need-fulfilling periods are usually the first to suffer; for example, in day care centers, meals, naptimes, and end-of-the-long-day periods are chronically beset with difficulties. Next, the newly acquired interests in people and activities forfeit pleasurable investment. The children wander around listlessly, disregard or misuse toys, and, directly or indirectly, demand mothering care or fall back on their self-comforting habits.

BABY-SITTING WITH SCHOOL-AGE CHILDREN

Except in situations of illness or severe stress, children from about six to eleven years of age are truly masters of their daily bodily needs. In fact, this aspect of their lives is relatively so independent of the relationship with the mothering person that a meal prepared differently or one that includes new foods may be quite welcome. They also enjoy a variety of relationships, activities, and interests which are satisfying in themselves. These developmental changes give the sitter a chance to build individual specific relationships with the children which are mutually enjoyable. It is no longer necessary to be as much like mother as possible in many areas. In baby-sitting with children in this age group it is very evident that the role of the parent–child relationship has shifted. Almost imperceptibly over the years, need fulfillment and learning to take care of one's needs, getting to be a person in one's own right, and functioning independently have receded into the background. Instead, the parent–child relationship serves to help the child build and maintain inner controls over his wishes and feelings and assists him in conforming to rules that affect not only his safety but ways of living with others according to family and community expectations. The parent substitute is usually so busy with these aspects that he or she barely notices the absence of demands for need fulfillment and the diminished stress of missing mother. In some ways the current responsibilities may seem bigger: "You can't play soccer in the neighbor's yard"; "You can't bike down to the drugstore"; "No, your friend can't stay for dinner and sleep over." Obviously, these changes do not mean that parents are no longer necessary or that the relationship with them is less important. Schoolchildren need their parents and miss them, but in different ways. In order to understand them better we shall have to follow the changing course of the parent–child relationship and its effect on the child's personality growth.

Competent baby-sitters know intuitively that their relationship with the child has to approximate the age-appropriate role of the parents' relationship. With very young children this means being familiar and consistent with the mother's ways of fulfilling needs and being aware of the stress of separation. With older children the task includes establishing the kind of relationship that will enable them to accept the sitter as the representative of the family's rules of living. When sitters have the time and the know-how to build this kind of relationship, they are trusted and can work in harmony with the children's expectations of themselves. "Look, you and I know that your parents don't think it's right to go to the playground after dinner. I wouldn't be a good sitter if I let you go and you wouldn't feel good about it either in the end. So let's just have a game at home." When, however, the sitter is strange to the children, unfamiliar with their usual routines and standards, and unskilled at forming the right kind of relationship, she is apt to find herself in the midst of chaos—a situation similar to that of being an inexperienced elementary school substitute teacher who is suddenly put into the void left by the absence of the familiar class teacher.

AREN'T ALL CHILDREN, EVEN VERY YOUNG ONES, SOMETIMES GLAD TO BE AWAY FROM THEIR PARENTS?

When children are old and competent enough not to need a sitter they can genuinely enjoy being away from their parents. To some extent this also applies to school-age children who enjoy varied relationships and activities, who like to practice and test their independence, and who have learned to combine appropriately the demands of their own conscience with the idea that, to a certain extent, different situations and groups operate on their own sets of rules and expectations. For example, it's okay to run around and yell in a neighborhood ball game but not at school or at the store. Also, it is always easier for children to leave their parents and know they are there to return to, than to be left by them.

With some older, and most younger children, however, the wish to get away from the parents and their rules may stem from different motives. With toddlers, as with Sandra in our earlier baby-sitting example, the wish to leave mother, to demonstrate how little one needs her, and to tease her even by turning lovingly to others, are part and parcel of the relationship with the mother. The child can enjoy it as long as he can be sure that he can return to her any time, and the reunion is as much a part of his toddler love and need as is the getting away.

Toddlers, and older youngsters even more so, also often want to leave mother as a way of paying her back for having been left by her The more they have felt helpless, hurt, and angry by her real or imagined "disloyalty" in leaving them, the more they apparently relish their chance to turn away to supposedly "better" people and things. Instances of this kind of reaction can be observed in most nurseries or day care centers. There are usually one or more children who could barely wait for the end of the school day, but when mother finally comes to get them they keep her waiting. Under the pretext of having to play with just one more toy, dawdling over dressing, or talking to others, they manage to convey to mother just how frustrating it is to be left unnoticed while your loved one is busy. Most mothers become quite irritated, but some understand and say, "I guess it's been a long time. I missed you too" (E. Furman, 1984, 1992b, 1993).

At a later point, the same behavior can even represent a way of being like the parents. For example, Kevin's parents were usually thrilled to go out, ready to "have a ball." He gathered from their remarks that they left behind not only their children but also their usual ways of behaving. In time he, like they, felt it was a mark of being grown up to want to "get away from it all" and shed the restrictions of family life.

Whereas these and other factors may contribute to the children's not-so-genuine enjoyment of being without the parents, it is also true that children have many impulses which they have not yet learned to curb or modify and which cause more or less conflict in the parent–child relationship. When the children resent the parental rules and restrictions, they sometimes hope to indulge themselves without their supervision. They may want to eat different kinds or quantities of food, watch forbidden TV programs, play excited games or hit one another; in short, when the cat's away, the mice can play. The baby-sitter who allows the children this kind of fun may be welcomed at the time but may not have an opportunity to witness the less happy aftermath, when the children's own guilt or the parents' disapproval catches up with them. As one child put it, "It was short-run fun but long-run misery."

4
The Early Father–Child Relationship

In some societies the paternal and maternal roles and functions are clearly defined by custom and law, leaving little or no leeway for individual variations. In other societies, or at other times within the same society, the lines of responsibility are less rigidly drawn, allowing much room for familial and personal preference. In our Western postindustrial culture patterns, earlier widely accepted models of parenting have undergone considerable change during this century. Related customs and laws are in a state of flux and many different ways of parenting are socially recognized and accepted. This has given groups, families, and individuals a new freedom of choice and opportunity to renovate the fabric of society. It has also burdened us with the need to make choices and to evaluate their effects.

Many of us have struggled to adapt to these societal changes and have attempted to meet our society's demand on us to come up with individual "rules" of parenting. Faced with this task we have felt a greater need than before to explore and understand human nature and the child's psychological requirements. Does a child need a mother and a father? Does each parent have specific roles to fulfill? What happens when mother and father reverse roles or share them equally? Some hope that a father's participation in the baby's earliest bodily care will make him a closer and more meaningful person to the child. Others feel that he will become less important when he ceases to be the family disciplinarian and wage earner. And others yet consider father redundant if mother can provide for her child, or mother redundant if father assumes the task of child care.

As we come to understand better some of the basic patterns and progressions of human mental growth and clarify for ourselves the facilitating roles of the environment, we may be able to answer some of these questions for ourselves to some extent. However, our answers will not provide us with ready prescriptions for bringing up children or for shaping societies. Since parenting is a complex psychological process, rather than a scientific endeavor, a mother's and father's knowledge of child development, however well versed they may be, is at best a helpful contributing factor. Its usefulness will depend on the way in which they integrate it into the other important determinants of their parenting: their individual personalities, past and present experiences, and actual interactions with each child—all within the context of their society.

With this in mind, let us consider our discussions of the child's changing needs and of his interactions with his parents and others as explorations of human growth, not as recipes for child rearing or as norms for an ideal society.

THE FATHER'S ROLE WITH HIS BABY

We have already touched on the development and nature of the father's role. We noted that through his relationship with the mother and their joint anticipation of the baby's birth he may invest his infant mentally as a part of himself already during the months of pregnancy. In that sense the beginning of his relationship with his child is similar to and yet different from that of the mother, who includes the child as a bodily as well as a mental part of herself.

As we then followed the development of the mother–child relationship in babyhood, we focused on its close connection with the mother's ongoing care of the baby's bodily needs and the baby's pleasurable experience of being cared for, an interaction which enables the baby to get to know and like both himself and her. We mentioned that during these early months of the baby's life the most important aspects of the father's role are his devotion to the mother–baby unit, his protectiveness of them, and his support for and appreciation of the mother's care of the baby. This helps her to fulfill her task, to enjoy it, and to find it worthwhile. Caring for a baby absorbs a mother in an endless succession of little details, most of which may seem insignificant or even distasteful to adults who are not involved with babies: the way the infant nurses, the hours he sleeps, the times he seems to have a tummy ache, how and when to bathe him, the color and consistency of his bowel movements, whether the new diapers cause him a rash, whether he spits up when he is helped to burp, and many more. Usually, nobody but the father can share the mother's interest in these events, listen to her accounts of the baby's activities, empathize with her concerns, and appreciate her efforts, because only he has a similar and shared loving investment in their child. However, just because infant care is so absorbing and so focused on primitive bodily concerns, the mother also needs the father's adult companionship. He talks with her about people and events outside the home, shares his thoughts about them, asks her for her views, and appreciates her contribution to their joint adult concerns. In doing so he enriches her life and helps her to regain an appropriate inner balance. When mothers cannot avail themselves of the father's mental support for their care of the baby and when he cannot fulfill their needs for adult companionship, it becomes very difficult for them to devote themselves to their babies. Some mothers then tend to become low in spirits, dissatisfied with themselves, and withdrawn or morose with their babies. Others take flight into activities and interests away from their babies. In either case, their mothering is impaired and their enjoyment of it diminished.

How about helping her with the care of the baby? A father may like to assist the mother by being the baby's occasional or regular baby-sitter. During the infant's first months this does not help him or the child to form a specific relationship. It also does not help the mother to enjoy mothering more, unless it happens in addition to, not instead of, the father's support and appreciation of her task. This is similar to other situations in our lives when we find ourselves confronted with a new and demanding task. When someone we care about takes an interest in our struggles, it helps us to persevere, to master it, and to gain satisfaction from it. It helps us much less in the long run when that person simply takes over the job at times, either with the idea of relieving us of an unpleasant chore or to show us how much better he can do it.

We have also already discussed the fact that, in the latter half of the first year, the well-developed infant begins to form specific new relationships in addition to the now well-established relationship with the mother. Fathers and siblings are usually the first to whom the baby's interest turns. They are well known to the child because he has been with them so often in the mother's presence and has observed her friendly contact with them. The most meaningful beginnings of these new relationships indeed take place from the safety of mother's arms or lap or while she feeds, bathes, or cleans the baby. During these times the infant watches Dad sitting nearby, touches brother's face, or laughs at sister's somersaults. The interested and available father then soon develops special interactions with the now older baby which are enjoyed by both: a finger game, a song, a chance to hold Dad's pen or to touch his watch, to chew on his jacket buttons, ride on his knees. The father's participation in the baby's bodily care does not enhance or speed up this new relationship. Father as mother-substitute is different from father as a loved person in his own right. Far from becoming "spoiled" by mother's continuous care, the baby's trusting experience of it actually furthers his mental growth and enables him to seek and enjoy new relationships all the sooner (Burlingham, 1973).

THE FATHER'S RELATIONSHIP WITH HIS TODDLER

As the infant grows into a toddler he acquires new functions which help him to be less dependent on his mother and to approach the father actively. Through self-feeding and enjoyment of a variety of foods he joins the family meal and asks for bits of what mother as well as father eat; by walking and running he can seek out Dad and climb onto his knees; with the help of his beginning use and understanding of speech he can engage father in verbal communication. The diminishing urgency of his needs and the ability to keep mother with him in mind because he now carries a loved mental image of her make it possible for the toddler to leave mother for short periods and to participate in more advanced father–child activities: driving to the drugstore to get the Sunday newspaper, going for a walk up and down the street, riding on Dad's shoulders or in the stroller, rolling the ball to and fro, getting in the way while Dad cleans the car, looking at a book together. Many of us can recall one or another such activity with our fathers from the later preschool years, although we are likely to have forgotten its beginnings when we were one-and-a-half or two years old (E. Furman, 1992b, 1993).

In this additional and separate relationship the father is spared the full impact of the toddler's relationship with his mother, his clinging possessiveness and provocative rebellion, his fierce controlling love and quick explosive anger, his testing and teasing. When the mother is the main recipient of this tyrannical toddler love she can best help the child to grow beyond it toward a more mature considerate relationship, for which the less intense and less conflictual bond with father already acts as an incentive. By contrast, when the father regularly doubles as mother, the toddler relates to both of them in his stormy, contrary way and finds it harder to leave it behind and to become considerate toward loved people.

WHY ARE TODDLERS INCONSIDERATE AND HOW ARE THEY HELPED TO CHANGE?

The toddler's close but primitive relationship with the mothering person contains a kind of love which derives pleasure not only from mutual kindness but also from mutual irritation and conflict. The child actually enjoys doing and saying teasy or contrary things that will "rile mother up," "get her goat," draw her into an excited interplay, or reduce her to helplessness and an ensuing struggle for power. At times, hurting and being hurt are sought and felt as a form of being intensely close to each other. We see remnants of this kind of loving in the later, more or less good-natured teasing between people who like one another, or in the intense arguments and fights of couples who are, in this way, closely bound to one another, or in people who feel that something is missing in life when there is no chance for a good old fight.

However, not all of the child's contrariness and lack of consideration stem from his special way of loving. His anger too is primitive and unmitigated in response to the slightest frustration. Mother's "no" to the child's demands, her leaving of him or inattention to him, her inability to arrange life according to his wishes, all are experienced as intolerable, deliberate insults or injuries deserving of total rejection or banishment. This is even true when the mother's restrictions are imposed for the sake of the child's safety and well-being ("No, you mustn't climb on the window"; "No, you may not put stones in your mouth"), or when circumstances beyond her control make it impossible to meet the child's demands. For example, she cannot change the weather so that the child can play in the sandbox, nor can she avoid leaving him with a sitter when she has to keep a doctor's appointment. In his angry frustration the toddler does not hesitate to wish mother away, to turn his love to others in the hope that they will prove more compliant, or to attack her and her things in an outburst of temper. He may even "punish" her by doing things to himself which he knows worry her, such as not eating, messing in his pants, or running into the street or other unsafe places. At these times the child's love and need of mother are temporarily forgotten. His actions distress him only later when he wants her again and fears that she may retaliate in kind and not be available to him.

As long as the mother remains the main continuous caring person, the child learns that his angry wishes do not materialize (she stays although he sends her away), that mother's ability to provide satisfactions outweighs the moments when she frustrates, and that she does not retaliate in kind but continues to love and protect her child even though she gets angry at him at times. He also learns that, at least most of the time, she does not respond with angry excitement to her child's provocations and does not share his fun in teasing, arguing, and fighting but prefers a more mature way of showing love. These experiences and mother's model help the child toward giving up his demands for loving–hurting tug-of-wars and toward achieving a new way of toning down hate or anger for the sake of love. He will not stop getting angry but, like mother, will begin to temper the nature of his anger in such a way as to preserve his love and his loved one in spite of it. "I am very angry at you but I still care about you and won't harm you." It is a difficult and slow process, determined by many factors but dependent above all on the relationship with the mothering person (E. Furman, 1992b, 1993).

HOW DOES THE FATHER HELP HIS TODDLER WITH THIS STEP?

The father's newly developing specific relationship with his child usually centers on activities which do not involve bodily needs or bodily pleasures. They involve the child's interest in experiences outside himself, offering glimpses of the world at large. The toddler finds a new kind of enjoyment in them, looks forward to them, and is eager to repeat them. They serve as an incentive to branch out from the intense mutually focused interaction with the mother. They are a taste of things to come and whet the appetite for growing up. The times with father may also serve as a respite for child and mother.

Caring for a toddler is, in many ways, even harder than caring for a baby. Mothers need occasional little breathers. The toddler's twenty minute walk or quiet play with Dad can be heaven when dinner is to be got ready. As during the child's babyhood, the father's support and appreciation of the mother's task is vital, both privately and in front of the child. He helps mother and child a great deal when he praises what she does ("That's a fine dinner Mom made"; "I like your nice new shoes. That was kind of Mom to buy them for you"), when he stands by her rules ("Mom says it's nighttime, so we have to stop now"), when he refuses to be hoodwinked into playing the better parent ("No, if Mom doesn't let you have candies now, I won't either"). Moreover, the father's considerate, appreciative behavior toward the mother as well as toward the child sets up a helpful model of what a more mature relationship is about. For the mother this adult relationship, and the companionship it entails, provide the necessary antidote to her life with the toddler and a perspective on its stresses. In short, the father's help, once again, enables her to be a good mother (R. A. Furman, 1983).

The father's role is both important and difficult to fulfill. With the provocative, forever-on-the-go toddler, it is all too easy to be critical of the mother, to minimize her job, and to refuse to help out, or to take over and "do better" (for a couple of hours). It is also tempting to join the toddler at his level, such as by playing excited games of tussling, tickling, and chasing, and then hand back to mother a thoroughly overstimulated child who will ultimately vent his excess tension in irritability at her. It is much harder to find calm, age-appropriate activities.

CAN A STEPFATHER OR OTHER PERSON SUBSTITUTE FOR THE BIOLOGICAL FATHER WITH THE TODDLER?

As far as the child is concerned, his need for additional relationships can be met by a variety of other household members—older siblings, grandparents, uncles. Stepfathers, adoptive fathers, and foster fathers can often invest themselves fully in their paternal relationship with the child and love him as if he were their own, because it is a mental rather than bodily bond. By the same token, some biological fathers may not be able to develop their relationship with the child, either through lack of opportunity or due to psychological interferences in their personalities (E. Furman and R. A. Furman, 1989).

The other aspect of the father's role, namely, that of supporting and assisting the child's mother in her task, can sometimes also be fulfilled by nonbiological fathers, but this is more difficult for them. If it isn't possible, this represents a big loss, directly to the mother, indirectly to the child (E. Furman, 1992a).

CAN MOTHER AND FATHER REVERSE ROLES VIS-À-VIS THEIR TODDLER?

As far as the toddler's well-being and development are concerned, it does not matter who fulfills the main caring role and

provides the opportunity for the ongoing one-to-one relationship. The difficulty lies with the adult. With toddlers, though
to a lesser extent than with babies, the capacity for investing
oneself fully in the child's care, empathizing with his feelings,
and meeting needs is usually easiest for the biological mother
for whom the child still represents a bodily part of herself or
for the woman (adoptive mother, stepmother, grandmother)
who has mothered the child during his first year and made him
her own with the help of her special motivation. A father usually has neither the natural mother's close bodily bond with
the child nor the adoptive mother's special motivation and pre-
ceding first year experience. However, under exceptional circumstances these handicaps could be overcome to a sufficient
extent: for example, if the father has been the primary caregiver from the very start.

WHAT HAPPENS WHEN BOTH MOTHER AND
FATHER SHARE IN THE TODDLER'S CARE?

We have already talked about the father as a baby-sitter and
the father as the provider of an additional relationship which,
in contrast to the primary relationship with the mothering
person, is focused more on enjoying joint activities and less on
bodily need-fulfilling care. When the father shares equally or
substantially in the ongoing care, his toddler relates to him
more like a second mother. His youngster receives "double" or
"split" mothering, an arrangement similar to the alternating
care by mother and nanny, mother and grandmother, or mother
and professional substitute, such as a day care worker. The
changeover in care may follow the child's wishes ("Today I want
Daddy to stay with me—to put me to bed—to stay at home with
me") or, as is mostly the case, it occurs according to the adults'
needs and convenience.

How does alternating mothering feel to the child and how
does it affect his ability to master phase-appropriate developmental tasks? Those of us who have worked with such families during the child's toddler years and have traced the effects
of shared care through treatment of the child at a later age
appreciate that this is a big topic and too full of individual

variations to do it justice in a brief discussion. But we can at least look at some outstanding general features, keeping in mind that "general" is not necessarily "individual" (E. Furman, 1984).

Perhaps the most obvious thing is that the mothering father invites and receives the same fiercely loving and conflicted investment as the mother and, at the same time, loses out on providing the important special additional relationship. The child now has to outgrow double the amount of gratification, and has less incentive to progress toward newly satisfying relationships because there is no different relationship with the father to pave the way. Sometimes this handicaps the child's later relationships. He continues to relate to others as though they were mothers and he were a toddler.

However, having two mothers is not more gratifying in all respects. When the toddler is with one parent, he does not have the other, either because he dismissed one parent in favor of the other or because he was left by him or her. One of the main tasks of this phase is to take over bodily self-care, to become mother to oneself, in toileting, dressing, or self-feeding. The child with one mother accomplishes this by "leaving" the mother figuratively to do for himself while counting on her continuous availability, much as later on adolescents venture out into the world but rely on the old home being there to touch base with in case of need. The mother's role is to be there to be left (E. Furman, 1982, 1994a). By contrast, the child who is left by the mother cannot count on her being there, and this makes becoming independent harder. Likewise, the child who "sends her away" and turns to his other mother or mothering father for care is not on the way to independence, but intent on changing mothers. Children with double mothering often lag in their wish to care for themselves. The changes in caregiver tend to make it more desirable to preserve the being-taken-care-of relationship than to relinquish it for the sake of independence. These children sometimes have to be cajoled or pushed to do for themselves and regard self-care as a chore instead of preferring to be masters of their bodies and resenting it when the adults don't let them ("Me do, me do").

Double mothering also makes it more difficult for the toddler to cope with angry feelings and to achieve that most important step of taming anger for the sake of love, which makes consideration for others possible. The child who controls which parent should care for him enjoys the power of summoning the current favorite and banishing the one he currently dislikes. But this does not help him to learn to accept and get along with the parent even when he is angry at him or her ("I'm mad at you, but I still love you enough to want to keep you and even to forgive you"). Nor does it help him to cope with the inevitable times when the parent has to leave him, a fact he is then apt to interpret along the lines of his own experience: "He leaves me because he doesn't want me, doesn't like me, or wants someone else more"—a scary and unsettling thought. It makes the child dread the parent's anger as much as he enjoys the omnipotence of his own anger, and it thwarts realistic understanding of the many reasons for leaving and being left. When the decision about who takes care is in the adults' hands, the toddler feels forever frustrated in his longing, and helpless to influence or bring about the closeness of his loved ones. Loving two mothers also means missing both and resenting the absence of either. This immeasurably increases the child's anger and makes it once again, though now for different reasons, harder to tame (E. Furman, 1992b, 1993).

Another reason why shared care makes it harder for the toddler to master the conflict of loving and hating the same person is that the similar relationship with two people invites splitting them up into a good one and a bad one. The "good" one receives all the love and is invested with all the virtues, the "bad" one gets all the hate, can't do anything right, and is blamed. Such a division of loving and hating may switch at a moment of frustration from one parent to the other, but it may also lead to permanent preferences and difficulty in liking people according to their real merits. Both like and dislike are, in these instances, based not only on what the parent actually does but on the opportunity to divert anger to someone else instead of modifying it and tempering it with love. In fairy tales and Westerns we reexperience these early solutions to loving and hating in our attitudes to the all-good and all-bad characters, the "good guys" and the "bad guys." In real life it is not helpful when we need to safeguard our love and loved ones at the cost of hatred for others. When we cannot rely on our love for others to hold the fort against damaging anger, we also cannot trust that others can truly love us. Such unresolved toddler conflicts are not always the outcome of equal care by two mothering persons. They can also result from other experiences, such as separations over longer periods or a relationship with a mother who herself suffers from this difficulty and cannot tame her anger at her child out of love for him.

The child who remains plagued by unmastered mixed feelings may later experience difficulty in separating from his parents and in enjoying relationships with others.

As a toddler Jane had been cared for by mother and father in alternating shifts due to the parents' work schedule. At that time she showed most difficulty when both parents were at home. She would either play up one against the other or was irritable and unhappy unless she commanded both parents' full presence and attention. She was very slow to become clean and had wetting and soiling accidents for a long time. She also did not like to dress herself and went about it so slowly that it often ended up being the parent's job. When Jane started nursery school at four years, she clung to her mother. For many weeks she could not feel comfortable at school without her and could not allow herself to like her teacher or to enjoy the school activities. She worried that mother might not come to pick her up and that mother might enjoy herself without Jane so much that she would prefer to stay away. At home, however, Jane spoke of nursery school in glowing terms and wished she could go to school on weekends and holidays. Whenever she felt dissatisfied with mother she declared that the teachers were much nicer and the school toys were much more fun. In working with Jane and her family on this difficulty we learned that Jane's unresolved feelings about mother's and father's alternating care now affected her relationship to home and school. She viewed the teacher as a second mother rather than as a person with whom she could form a special additional relationship. At home, when she was assured of mother's presence, she vented her anger by stating her wish for that second "better" teacher–mother; at school she warded off her temptation to be disloyal to mother by not allowing herself to enjoy school, and was plagued with concern that mother would be disloyal to her and abandon her. She expected her mother would get rid of her if she proved unsatisfying, just as she, Jane, wanted to exchange mothers when her mother displeased her. Jane had failed to temper her toddler anger, had not yet learned to love a person even though she got angry at him or her at times.

Shared care does not have to produce adverse effects. When the parents are aware of the stresses and potential pitfalls it entails, they can help to minimize and overcome them There are many ways to do that. For example, it helps when one parent takes the role of sitter and supports the child's relationship with the main mothering person; it helps when times of absences and takeover are regular and prepared for so that the child always knows what to expect, feels less helpless and angry; most importantly, it helps when the parents can feel with the child and assist him in recognizing and expressing his anger, sadness and other feelings about the arrangements so that he can better master them.

WHAT HAPPENS TO THE TODDLER'S RELATIONSHIPS WHEN HIS CARE IS SHARED EQUALLY BY SEVERAL PEOPLE?

Sometimes this means that others help with the care in the presence of the mother, so that she retains the primary relationship with her child, as in a big household. The child can then turn back to her at all times and treats the others as part substitutes and part additional persons to relate to. Even when the mother is not always there, she may still remain the main caregiver whose relationship helps to mitigate the stress of changes and separations. In extreme instances of multiple care, however, there is a danger that the child's relationships will be spread so thinly that none of them will be sufficiently close and meaningful to influence the toddler's mental growth, to help him overcome his primitive self-interest and intolerance, to modify his anger, and develop appropriate concern for others. Children who become arrested at this developmental point may never be able to maintain a mutually caring or trusting relationship and may act on their sadistic or violent impulses for personal gains, for perverse satisfaction, or in response to frustration. This makes it difficult for them to maintain a marital relationship or to parent consistently, may lead to spouse and child abuse, and may jeopardize adjustment to the wider social community. Some adult psychopathic criminals suffer from this kind of pathology, as illustrated, for example, in Truman Capote's book *In Cold Blood* (1965). With young delinquents of this type the most effective correction lies in providing a new opportunity for a close long-term relationship which may, belatedly, fulfill the parental role with the toddler. Such help consists of many years of skilled devotion, but may prove only partially effective. It is not known exactly at which point a person can still benefit and correct earlier deficits. There are many individual variations. In general, the younger the child, the better the outlook.

Similar difficulties may result from serious disruptions or inadequacies in the toddler's relationships, such as when the mothering person is permanently lost without adequate replacement, or when the continuous caring person provides insufficient loving experiences for the child (Aichhorn, 1925; Bowlby, 1944; Friedlander, 1947).

5

Mother–Father–Child

THE YOUNG PRESCHOOLER AND HIS PARENTS

As the two-year-old toddler gradually grows into a three- to four-year-old preschooler, the nature of his relationships changes and they serve new functions in the child's developing personality. Needs become less urgent and the preschooler is more able to meet them on his own, be it getting a drink of water, putting on his coat and shoes, or tolerating a feeling. He also considers himself more clearly and stably a person in his own right. Bodily and mental dependency cease to be the main tie to the loved one. The child becomes more interested in people as people: how they look, what they do, and how he compares to them. Mother and father now assume a new and more equal importance and meaning in the child's life, and their roles change.

Even in casual encounters, preschoolers impress us with their intense personal curiosity about people and with their spontaneity in sharing equally personal information about themselves.

Accompanying her mother at the supermarket, three-year-old Jenny suddenly asked the checkout clerk, "Are you a mommy?" When the startled woman replied that she had two children, Jenny upstaged her with, "We have lots of children—me and John and Bill and my mommy even has a baby."

At the bus stop, four-year-old Jeremy observed to his dad in a loud whisper, "Why does that man have a cane? Is he a grandpa?"

In the doctor's waiting room Heather told everyone that she was going to get a shot with her checkup. The one woman who evinced interest was treated to additional impressive news, "And my sister got her shot last week. And I got a big doll for Christmas and she makes wee-wee if you put water in her. And these are my new shoes," and Heather showed them off to good advantage.

Some people are put off by the children's lack of respect for privacy, some react defensively, especially when the child's observation or question exposes their vulnerable spots, but many people sense that the youngster invites them to participate in a specific way of relating—a kind of mutual admiration society—and they respond in kind. When a nursery school teacher, attuned to this kind of relationship, meets a new pupil, she usually says something like "I am glad to meet you, Charlie, you have very handsome big cowboy boots on. I bet they are quite new." Or, "So you are Susan. Your mommy told me about you and I like the blue ribbons in your hair." And while Charlie or Susan beam coyly, the teacher generally proceeds to show off a bit herself and invites the child's admiration, "Now we have some very nice toys here for you to see. You might especially like our big new blocks in the corner here and the dollhouse over there."

Wherever preschoolers live, play, and learn, their focus is on watching and finding out what others are about and on drawing their admiring attention: "Look at me"; "See how high I can jump"; "I have the biggest ball." This type of behavior is so commonplace that we often take it for granted and do not fully appreciate that it represents a phase-specific way of loving and being loved which would strike us as inappropriate if we encountered more than a touch of it in the relationships of adults. (Can you imagine the nursery school teacher meeting the child's mother with a comment on *her* clothes?) We are not even surprised when the youngster's unhappiness with or anger at his loved ones manifest themselves in the same vein; when he feels envious and inadequate in the face of their prowess or when he tries to inflict these feelings on them by boosting himself up a notch: "*You* don't even get to go to her party!"; "My candy is bigger than yours"; "Our car is more fancy."

Inevitably, gratifying one's curiosity entails opportunities to make comparisons which may arouse admiration or envy, or cause blows to one's self-esteem. How intense such feelings are and how well they can be tolerated and mastered depends on whether one also feels appreciated and loved for one's own qualities ("Yes, John is a very good ballplayer but you are especially good at block building. That house you built yesterday was just great"), whether one is allowed, or even invited, to share in the other person's desirable attributes ("I got a new board game and *you* can play it with me"), and whether one can see one's way to achieving the same or similar accomplishment ("I've been cutting out cookies for a long time and that's why I'm so good at it, but now you can start practicing and you'll see that very soon yours will turn out very well too. Look at this last one. It is much better than the one you did before."). The more chances there are for becoming like loved, admired persons or to share in their desirable "greatness," and the more their appreciation of one's own qualities helps to soften the hardship of one's envy and inadequacy, the more gratifying is the relationship of the "mutual admiration society" and the better it serves its functions in the preschooler's personality growth: to provide knowledge about the world, models to emulate, and ways of making them a part of oneself. It is in the nature of this and to some extent of all relationships that when we love and admire someone very much we want to become like him or her, at least in some respects. Many of our attitudes, interests, values, and ideas stem from identifications with loved, admired persons. Most of us remember, perhaps from a later period in our lives, a friend or beloved teacher who instilled in us the beginning of a new interest or way of looking at life which have now long since become an integral part of ourselves. Some of us also remember occasions when the wished-for ideal seemed all too far away and hopelessly unattainable. In this vein a young woman recalled a commercial for cameras which she used to watch as a four-year-old. It showed next to one another a snapshot of a little girl with her doll, then one of her graduating from college in full regalia, and finally one of her wedding where she appeared in white, accompanied by her handsome groom. "I watched it over and over," she commented, "and wished so desperately that I could get there just as fast. It seemed that for me it took forever."

Of course, some changes lie far in the future and some things one can never have for oneself. It is very difficult for young children to content themselves with having to wait or with having to do without altogether and still be able to enjoy what they are and have now. This is especially true when the youngsters' curiosity and admiration focus on what is closest to home, namely their own bodily attributes and functions and those of their most important loved ones, their parents and perhaps siblings. We noted earlier that even babies perceive many of the differences between mother and father—their different looks, voices, smell, feel. The toddler's observations and experiences with his parents amplify and deepen this knowledge, and children early on start to compare themselves with the adults, often with painful awareness of their own helplessness and incompetence in contrast to the grown-ups' power and seeming perfection. During the preschool years the child becomes particularly aware of the sexual differences between people. Who is a man? Who is a woman? What is a boy? What is a girl? How are they alike and how do they differ? Understanding the facts is quite difficult, but it is perhaps even harder to accept and feel comfortable with one's own sexual identity and immaturity. Children inevitably perceive that others are not only differently endowed but may be bigger, stronger, and more capable. Although the little boy and girl may know in which ways they are like the adult of the same sex, the differences between boy and man, girl and woman, are almost as impressive as the differences between the sexes. Such discoveries pose a threat to the child's bodily and mental self-esteem and cause envy and anger. The child's concerns and misgivings may be helped by intellectual understanding, but they are tolerated and mastered only through the relationship with the parents (E. Furman, 1985a).

When we say, "The father shows a boy what a man is about," we mean that, in order for a boy to understand and like himself as a boy and to want to grow up to be a man and father, he has to have a father who enjoys being one and who serves as a model. Indeed it takes that, but also much more. The son's wish to adopt the paternal model depends very much on the nature of the father–child relationship and on the father's attitude to his son's manliness and growing up in all areas of daily living. If a boy is to feel that he wants to become a man, that he has a chance to reach this goal, and that he still amounts to something worthwhile now although he is little and less competent, he has to experience the kind of relationship that most ordinary, devoted fathers provide. He has to experience the mutual bond of shared activities in which the father enjoys and encourages the child's participation ("Hey, want to come and rake leaves with me? It's more fun when we do it together"), the trust that the father will help him learn the admired skills and appreciate the child's efforts and successes ("What a great job you're doing. You've really learned to handle that rake well"), and the opportunities for sharing in father's "greatness" ("Dad and I raked all the leaves"; or "My daddy can count to a thousand"; or "My dad won't let you bother me").

However, it is not only the relationship with the father and the model he offers that help a boy to consolidate and like his sexual identity. The mother's love of her boy and of her man are equally important.

Likewise, the little girl needs a supportive relationship with a mother who enjoys being a mother and a woman, and she needs a relationship with a father who loves and admires little girls. She too needs to know "What a man is about" in the widest sense. When a girl merely views a man as a person with a different body but lacks the context of a close relationship to know how he feels, thinks, and acts, she is much more likely to feel angry and deprived. Her self-esteem is immeasurably enhanced by his appreciation of her and of her achievements and by the opportunity to include him in her self-love: "*my* daddy" becomes a part of the "me" and lends it the sometimes essential boost at times of feeling inadequate.

Assisting the preschooler in consolidating and accepting his sexual identity and immaturity as well as helping the young child to develop new interests, skills, and goals are important functions of the relationship with both parents, but they are not the only ones. Actually, when we ask people what the parents' main role with their children is, they usually answer: "Make them mind"; "Discipline them"; "Tell them how to behave"; "Stop them from being naughty and getting into trouble." In other words, we tend to think of the areas in which the parents' and children's wishes conflict. And this happens quite often.

Sometimes it happens when the child wants very much to be like the parents but cannot bear to wait and acquire laboriously the necessary know-how (Johnny "borrows" Dad's pen and letter paper and scribbles busily, using up page after page—"just like Dad"), or when the child wants to be grown up in ways inappropriate to his mental or bodily capacities (Mary refuses to go to bed because she wants to join Mom and Dad at a concert; Brian insists on lifting the heavy shopping bag, like Dad, drops it and spills the contents). At other times the parent–child conflict arises from the child's need for independence and his wish to gratify his needs and impulses directly, immediately, and without interference ("I don't want to wait for dinner, I'm taking my cookies off the tray now"; "I want to play in the sandbox and I don't care if my clothes get all muddy"; "But I like to run around naked, it's fun!"; "I like to jump up and down on the couch, whee!"; "No, I won't stop and if you won't let me, *you'll* get it." And the parent often does "get it," in word and in deed).

It is said that education consists of "not this but that; not here but there; not now but later." Teaching and learning how to tolerate frustration, how to delay gratification, how to accept compromises and substitutes are a tall task for parents and children. We shall talk about its complexity in more detail later. Suffice it to say at this point that all measures are doomed to failure unless they are taken in the context of a close relationship. Its ties reward the young child's efforts and help him soften his resentment. Much hardship can be borne for the sake of gaining the parents' loving appreciation ("Now there's a good girl. It's hard to wait but I knew you could do it") and many a temptation can be resisted with the help of the parents' spoken, or implied, appeal to the child's wish to become like them ("*Daddy* waits for his dinner"; "*Bigger* children take care of their clothes").

THE OLDER PRESCHOOLER AND
HIS PARENTS

In time the preschooler's "mutual admiration society" bond with the parents also paves the way toward a new and more adult relationship with them. Thoughtful love for another person takes the place of the earlier self-centered demand for attention, and sexual and other differences between people serve as a source of attraction and pleasure rather than of discomfort and competition.

Five-year-olds and kindergartners often astonish us with their spontaneous helpfulness, which stems from genuine loving concern—"Mom, I cleaned up the playroom. I wanted to give you a nice surprise"; "Dad, you look tired. Did you have a hard day at the office? I'll get you the newspaper"; "Mom, I let Sally play with my blocks so she wouldn't bother you." Their occasional gifts begin to be chosen with a view to what the recipient might enjoy and bear less often the mark of seeking admiration for oneself. We are apt to hear, "I made you a picture for your kitchen so you have something to look at when you cook dinner," instead of the earlier, "Isn't this the best picture of a house you ever saw? You can have it." The change is neither sudden nor complete. Features of the child's earlier levels of relationship persist to some extent. The five-year-old still enjoys mother's fulfillment of his needs and her bodily and mental care. He still indulges in occasional teases and toddlerlike tugs-of-war, and there remains a good deal of wanting to impress others and be admired by them. But there is a new ability to give of oneself in love and to seek a partner to complement rather than to enhance oneself.

Father and mother become additionally significant in their roles as husband and wife. Children have now reached the point in development when, through their own feelings for each of the parents, they can understand the parents' mutuality, the complementary and cooperative nature of the marital relationship, the capacity to give to one another, and to create something jointly. This applies to the parents' sexual relationship and ability to make babies as well as to their many other activities: for example, the way they share and complement one another's daily tasks to make a home. The child not only likes to share in that relationship but may want now this, now that parent as his exclusive partner. It is frustrating and disappointing to feel left out of some aspects of the parental relationship, to experience the fact that two is company and three is a crowd, and to realize how one falls short compared to one's rival. Some of us recall such moments in our own lives. One young man related, "I used to always get into my parents' bed in the morning, right in the middle between them." One woman remembered how she always "hung on my daddy's arm," and another still felt half-pleased, half-ashamed for "talking a mile a minute so that mom and dad couldn't talk to each other."

When I once asked a group of high school seniors why a five-year-old girl needed a father, one woman student replied, "She needs him to learn what it is like to be loved by a man." Freud made a related comment many years ago: "A mother's task is to teach her son how to love." These are indeed important experiences. It is only when the child is thus loved that he or she can appreciate and come to terms with the fact that the parents' love for their son or daughter differs from their love for each other.

I should like to touch on another aspect of father's and mother's role, namely, how they combine within their own personalities, or complement in the relationship with one another, the universal bisexual elements which exist in each of us along with our specific sexual identity. It is widely recognized that men and women can usefully integrate their masculine and feminine, passive and active tendencies into their individual lives and activities; for example, men can find satisfaction in taking care of people (as fathers, physicians, nurses, chefs, etc.) and women can be efficient and effective with machinery (as drivers, engineers, scientists, etc.). Some societies restrict their members' opportunities for such activities (e.g., Kikuyu women are not allowed to hunt); others make definite provision for them (e.g., Samoan men do most of the cooking); and others yet expect each person to make full use of his or her individual potential. This latter pattern is becoming more prevalent in the United States and Europe. Our children observe that some mothers enjoy doing woodwork and others do not, some fathers like to prepare a meal and others do not. In their preschool years children begin to learn about these preferences in their parents, take part in many of the activities, and test which ones appeal to them.

It is sometimes thought that when a society restricts its members' activities according to their sexual identities (men can only do this, women can only do that), it imposes severe frustrations on the individual and may cause them to resent their sexual identity or to envy the other sex. It is often forgotten that we can achieve gratification not only by doing things ourselves but also by enjoying vicariously what others do.

When one young girl transferred from an all-girl to a coeducational elementary school, her parents asked her, after some time, how she liked her new school. She replied that it was wonderful because she now never needed to be naughty, the boys did it all for her and she could just sit back and enjoy it. Vicarious gratification assumes a special dimension when it occurs in the context of a close relationship. Many men gratify their femininity by gaining pleasure from their wives' lives— their appearance, activities, mothering, feeling, and thinking (R. A. Furman, 1983). Similarly, many women have for centuries gratified their masculine strivings through the lives of their fathers, husbands, and sons. Women who, by choice or necessity, restrict themselves to the roles of housewives and mothers are not *necessarily* frustrated, bitter, or depressed but may complement their direct satisfactions with those they indirectly experience in their closest relationships with their men. Pride in one's child's achievements is taken for granted; deep satisfaction in one's spouse's pursuits or accomplishments is equally possible. This is of course also true in areas that are quite unrelated to sexual identity or bisexual tendencies. Most of us are not "best" at everything and, although we may sometimes envy others their accomplishments or gifts, we often derive pleasure from their performances, be they artists, athletes, politicians, scientists, or just the clever man next door who always gets his roses to bloom. In the ordinary family, the parents' division of labor is not based on superiority and inferiority, or on strictly apportioned pseudo-equality, but derives naturally from what and how each can best contribute to the common goal of the whole family's well-being.

THE PASSING OF THE PRESCHOOL YEARS

Although children forget the specifics of these early impres-
sions, the feeling tone of their experiences with their parents as a couple and as father and mother remain with them,
become a part of themselves in the form of interests and goals,
ideals, and values, and affect their perceptions of themselves
and others. They determine, to a considerable extent, the
children's later comfort with themselves and with their sexu-
ality as well as their capacity to maintain satisfying relationships with men and women, to enjoy a marital bond and a
family, and to parent.

Whereas these effects become evident in the child's future
life, others manifest themselves in the present. Painful lessons
are learned of what the child can and cannot have now, of tolerating being left out of some aspects of the parental life, of
appreciating that one will have to wait a long time and master
many things before one can become adult like the parents.
Older now, and wiser, the child gives up some of his intense all-
consuming investment in his parents. His horizon widens to
include new relationships and new pursuits outside the immediate family. Teachers, friends, school, sports, and hobbies
become much more important and meaningful.

In this as in the earlier phases of the child's development,
the parent–child relationship serves a double role. On the one
hand it meets the child's current bodily and psychological needs,
on the other hand it becomes a building block in the growing
structure of the child's personality. This means that the child,
at each developmental level, gradually internalizes—takes into
himself—the parental function. What was done for and to him
becomes a part of himself. When the end of a developmental
phase is reached, the child becomes able to do for himself what
the parents used to do. In this way he comes closer to being an
adult with each step. Of course phases overlap and do not start
or finish on a certain day. The child's taking over of parental
functions and building his own personality takes place piecemeal and extends over a long period. By the time children are
ready for elementary school, they are able to take care of many
of their bodily needs, have established their sexual identity,
have acquired many skills, and mastered many tasks. Toward

the end of the preschool phase the child takes a particularly big step. He takes in the parental morals, their "rights and wrongs." These become the basis of his own conscience, of his standards for and judgments of himself. From this time on, and forever after, when we do something "right" (in accord with the demands of conscience), our conscience makes us feel good about ourselves, and when we do something "wrong," it makes us feel bad or guilty—even if nobody praises or scolds or even knows about the deed. Although the conscience is not an exact replica of the parental values, ideals, and admonitions, it does, to a considerable extent, represent them inside the child's mind, and this lessens his dependence on the "outside" parents. We shall discuss the conscience and its role again at a later point.

WHAT HAPPENS WHEN THE PRESCHOOLER'S MOTHERING OR FATHERING PERSON IS NOT THE BIOLOGICAL PARENT?

As we already know from our previous discussions, adoptive parents, stepparents, or foster parents can often invest themselves fully in the parental relationships with the child and substitute very adequately for the biological parent(s). We know also that some biological parents are unable to function as parents. When the nonbiological parents are also marital partners, it is particularly helpful to the child's development, allowing him or her to relate to them not only as mother and father but also as a couple. The preschooler, however, in contrast to the younger toddler, is likely to become aware of the reality that one or both of his parents are not his progenitors, even if he has never known the biological parents. His phase-appropriate curiosity about the functions of people's bodies, the origins of babies, and the relationships between people lead him to question and find out about his own history, or, if he knows it already, to intensify his interest. As the child learns the reasons for not living with his biological parents, he is usually confronted with sad or frightening events; for example, the biological parent died or was killed, or divorced from the marital partner, or was unable to parent and decided to find another home for the child. Such happenings may be painful and difficult to understand. They may be experienced as threatening and may increase the child's sense of being helpless because he had no control over them or, as one little boy put it, "And they didn't even ask my permission" (E. Furman, 1974; Wieder, 1977).

Although nothing can altogether obviate such distress, children can be helped to cope with it and master it sufficiently so that it does not impede their healthy progressive development. The best way is to help children through their trusting relationships with their substitute parents, who can discuss these matters with the child, assist him in understanding them, empathize with his hurt, and soothe it with their love (Krementz, 1982). It is a difficult task for substitute parents but one that serves to strengthen their relationships with the child as well as to help him. Experience has shown that in instances where children cannot ask their parents, or do not get truthful answers, or cannot get parental help with the mastery of facts and feelings, it is much harder for the children to come to terms with the realities, and their relationships with the substitute parents may suffer to an extent. This can be a great loss for the children and the substitute parents.

WHAT HAPPENS WHEN THE PRESCHOOLER HAS ONLY ONE PARENT?

In families where one parent has died, or permanently disappeared, the child is often helped very much by a substitute who maintains a relationship with the child and fulfills some of the absent parent's functions. For example, when there is no mother, an older sister, female relative, or housekeeper may take on this role, or when the father is deceased, an older brother, uncle, grandfather, or male friend of the family may be of help. Such substitute relationships provide opportunities for getting to know what a man or woman is "all about," they serve as models for identification, and they bolster the child's self-esteem by enabling him to share in their adult status. At best, however, the child still misses out on living with and learning about the parents' husband–wife relationship. This is a considerable loss for him at the time as well as for his future life and presents him with a special stress to overcome. There is also the additional stress of having to understand and cope with the reasons for the absence of the parent (R. A. Furman, 1980, 1983; E. Furman, 1983, 1992a, 1992b, 1993; E. Furman and R. A. Furman, 1989).

Children who cannot avail themselves of a substitute relationship have a much harder time. They miss out on the gratifications and functions of the relationships with parents of both sexes and often feel themselves diminished in comparison with more fortunate peers. In lieu of a realistic image of the unavailable mother or father, they fill in the gaps with their fantasies, which tend to picture the missing parent as ideal or potentially threatening, as too "good" or too "bad," or both.

Five-year-old Henry had initially been cared for by his unmarried mother, and from age one-and-a-half years on had lived in a small children's home, staffed entirely by women and located in isolation on the outskirts of a little village. He was well loved by the matron (director–nurse) who came rather close to being a substitute mother. However, he had hardly any access to men and no chance at all to relate to one. When I knew him, just after the Second World War, there was as yet no television, so that he rarely even saw pictures of men. Yet Henry talked about men almost constantly, in part asking about them, in part describing his vivid ideas about what they could or would do. The mailman, seen at a distance from the window, and the milkman, with whom he occasionally exchanged a greeting, became figures of great importance in Henry's life. Sometimes he fantasied that they would take him to their homes and lavish their love and gifts on him, but at other times he feared they would attack and hurt him or appear in the dark of night to frighten or kidnap him. At times he boasted about what he would be like when he grew up, the fantastic feats he would perform, and the unrealistic favors or punishments he would bestow on others. In reality Henry was quite lovable at times but lacking in self-control and quick to anger. He also was a bully—the mark of the child with little self-confidence. He attacked the weaker ones but became fearful and submissive when he knew or suspected that someone could really stand up to him.

Henry's situation was extreme but not unique. He and others like him helped me to recognize how great a thirst there is in children for the "other" parent, even when they are loved by one parent and when they have little opportunity to compare themselves with children in other families. It was also impressive to see how difficult it is for children to form a realistic idea of a man in the absence of real experience.

Usually children cared for by one parent have much more access to men and women and, given their own wish and the parent's permission or encouragement, it is easier for them to get to know people and to build relationships with them. The more satisfactory these turn out to be, the better it is for the child. However, some measure of stress is probably unavoidable (E. Furman, 1981b).

Andy's early experiences were more fortunate than Henry's, although he too was without a father, the latter having died when Andy was a baby. Andy lived with his devoted mother, who appreciated and supported his growing boyishness. She had loved her husband and often talked with Andy about his father so that the boy formed some idea of what his father had been like. They also discussed the father's death, and with his mother's help Andy learned to cope with the difficult facts and feelings related to it. Andy maintained a close relationship also with his grandfather, and the two enjoyed many activities and social times together. There were also many contacts with families of friends and less intimate experiences with people in the wider community. Andy became a well developed and capable three-and-a-half-year old, but on entering nursery school he experienced difficulty. He compared himself unfavorably to his boy peers. They appeared bigger, stronger, and more competent to him and he feared that he could neither compete with them nor be accepted and liked by them. In order to hide his presumed inferiority and to gain friends, he limited himself to copying the ideas and behavior of others, did not utilize his own abilities, and at times withdrew from activities altogether after half-hearted efforts. When other fathers visited or picked up their children, Andy either pretended not to notice or watched with wistful awe and longing. He reproached his mother for not providing a father for him, yet resented her attention to male friends. At the start of elementary school his standards for himself were unrealistically high, and when he inevitably failed to live up to them, his early conscience was very harsh. Guilt feelings lowered his self-esteem and self-confidence.

Single parent families due to separation or divorce vary greatly. In some the children continue to maintain close and satisfying relationships with both parents, in others they hardly ever see the parent who does not live in the home, in yet others the parents' remarriage requires that the children adapt to two families and several new siblings. The individual circumstances and relationships vary so much that it is impossible to generalize. It is fair to say, however, that the breakup of the husband–wife relationship and the dissonance between them constitute a special stress for the child (Wallerstein and Kelly, 1980; Goldstein and Solnit, 1984; E. Furman and R. A. Furman, 1989; E. Furman, 1991). It also constitutes a special and difficult task for the parents to help their child, to feel with him, and to understand his hardships at a time when each of them is embittered and upset or elated and relieved.

In general it is more difficult for children to feel good about themselves and to develop realistic inner standards and expectations when one parent is physically or emotionally unavailable to them (and this can even happen in two-parent families) and/or when the paternal and maternal figures do not maintain a marital relationship. When at least one parent recognizes that the situation is stressful for the child and is willing and able to help, these difficulties can be modified and mastered to a considerable extent. By contrast, the child's chances of a healthy development are further impeded when the parent(s) fail the child in this respect, either by denying the impact on the child or by expecting his feelings to be the same as theirs.

CAN A PERSON RAISED IN A FAMILY WITHOUT A HUSBAND–WIFE RELATIONSHIP HAVE ONE HIMSELF AND CAN HE BE A PROPER PARENT?

The child's experience of the parents' marital relationship plays an important part in the adult wish for and comfort with this kind of relationship, and the ability to parent indeed depends on having been parented, but these are not the only determining factors. Other early and later life experiences also matter, as well as each person's unique ways of coping with them. Early stresses may be overcome or compensated for and an individual's weak points in some areas may be balanced by strengths in other areas. Being able to maintain a relationship with a spouse and parenting are not all or none pursuits; at best they are not perfect. Sometimes an unhappy experience with two parents can cause as much or more difficulty as not having one parent.

In discussing this topic, one young man, in his late teens, related how distressed he was by his father's repeated mention of the fact that he, the father, had grown up without a father, had suffered much hardship because of it, but had worked extra hard and supported his bereaved family, and paid for his own education. Holding himself up as a model, the father complained that his son failed to achieve as well and did not make good use of the advantages he enjoyed. The son, our young man, felt sorry for his father's deprivation and bad about his own shortcomings but, he sighed, "My father had one great advantage that I never had. He didn't have a dad who was constantly criticizing him and telling him how lucky he was."

CAN ONE ESCAPE OR MODIFY WHAT IS PASSED ONTO ONESELF BY ONE'S PARENTS?

One cannot altogether escape what is passed on because the full development of one's personality depends on taking in aspects of one's parents. However, one need not take into oneself everything, and one can and does modify many features to a considerable extent. Moreover, we often take in what the parents seemed like to us or what we wished they were, rather than how they actually acted. No parent is perfect. Recognizing and accepting one's parents' fallibility, quirks, and unhelpful traits is an essential part of growing up, which starts already in the later preschool years. The parents often help the child with this process when they are aware of their shortcomings and encourage the child explicitly to avoid repeating them in their own personalities. ("I am not good at being punctual and it makes it so hard for me and for others. I hope you will be very different and much better in that way than I am.") Sometimes we become aware much later that we are just like our parents and can work at changing our attitudes. Often, what we have taken in from our parents is altered or overlaid by subsequent identifications with other people who have become very meaningful to us. But there are always some parental aspects, helpful and unhelpful, which we perpetuate in ourselves without even knowing them. However, it is also important to remind ourselves that we do not simply consist of what is passed on to us by our parents. Each person's individual endowment, his propensity to develop special gifts or to be subject to special deficits, also asserts itself and interacts with the environmental influences in such a way as to produce a unique personality.

WHAT HAPPENS TO THE PRESCHOOLER'S SEXUAL IDENTITY WHEN MOTHER AND FATHER REVERSE ROLES OR WHEN THEY KEEP STRICTLY TO MALE AND FEMALE "STEREOTYPED" ROLES?

A boy's or girl's sexual identity relates to gender, that is, the male or female characteristics and functions. They compare themselves in this respect to each other and to the adults. They learn that, as they grow up, they will come to be like the parent of their own gender. A person's gender is not determined by his activities, clothes, or manners, or by nonsexual bodily attributes, such as gait or facial expression. Such characteristics may be associated with masculinity or femininity in some societies or in the minds of some individuals, but they do not define sexual identity. We realize how true this is when we remind ourselves that a woman in pants may be a fully functioning wife and mother and that very manly Scottish men wear skirts. When little Mary tells us that her friend is a girl because she has long hair, we know that Mary either does not yet appreciate the real nature of sexual differences or prefers not to think of them.

A young child is helped to conceive correctly his or her own sexual identity by understanding what really makes a person a boy or a girl, a man or a woman. Children are helped to feel good about their sexual identity when both parents appreciate them for what they are and when the parent of their same sex feels comfortable with his or her own sexual identity. As long as this is the case, it does not matter whether the parents reverse roles in nonsexual activities or keep to "stereotypes." (E. Furman, 1985a).

The difficulty for the child arises when the parents are not comfortable with their sexual identities, when one or both feel inadequate as a man or a woman, or dissatisfied with his or her gender. When such emotional overtones determine a parent's insistence on or avoidance of certain activities, clothes, or other attributes, the parent conveys his or her inner discomfort to the child. Such parents are also likely to have difficulty in appreciating the child's sexual identity and in helping him or her to understand and value members of both sexes. Thus, the problem does not arise from whether mother or father fixes the car or washes the dishes, but from the way they feel about it in relation to their sexual identity. Children are very astute in sensing their parents' feelings and in responding to them.

THE ROLE OF THE PARENTS WITH THE OLDER CHILD

For the schoolchild and adolescent the parents remain essential figures. They not only provide for the growing individual's physical well-being but help consolidate and enrich the foundations of his emotional growth which they laid, almost single-handedly, during the child's earlier years: taking care of oneself, relating to others, establishing and maintaining ideals and values, acquiring interests and knowledge, learning new activities, and, eventually, growing away and becoming more than ever like the parents as a self-supporting adult with a mate and family of his own.

In the child's mind, however, the parents, from school age on, lose some of their earlier all-absorbing significance and intense emotional investment. People and activities outside the immediate family circle increasingly gain in importance and contribute their share to the development of the child's personality (A. Freud, 1958; R. A. Furman, 1983).

6
Friends and Relatives

WHAT IS A FRIEND?

Many of us know what it feels like to have a friend, yet when we are asked to define it we often falter. "A friend is someone who helps you when you are in need, who keeps you company when you feel lonely, who stands up for you when others are against you, who listens to your troubles, who visits you when you are sick, who loves you in spite of your shortcomings." Yes, but so does a mother. Isn't there a difference? "Oh yes, a friend does more. He enjoys things you enjoy, he shares some of your interests and activities, he goes to the movies with you or to a party." Yes, but so does a companion, a colleague, an acquaintance, even a parent or sibling. "But a friend is more someone your own age, a peer." Yes, but a peer is not necessarily a friend and a friend need not be a peer. Indeed, a friend is all these things and can be of any age—someone who can empathize and sympathize with our feelings, who shares some of our interests and activities, who helps and supports us even when it causes him inconvenience or requires some self-sacrifice. But surely the most important characteristic of a friendship is its mutuality, the fact that we do all these same things for our friend. This sustained give and take, this reciprocity, distinguishes a friendship from all other relationships and as such requires a considerable degree of emotional maturity in each partner.

WHEN CAN ONE BEGIN TO HAVE A FRIEND?

Babies certainly can't make friends. They may be intently interested in other babies, stare at them, follow their movements, even smile at them, but they do not turn to another baby for help or comfort, do not extend themselves to others, and would not even be able to engage in a joint game. Toddlers sometimes enjoy playing alongside another child. In a sandbox, and with mother safely nearby, two or even three toddlers may fill and dump their buckets, quietly aware of and content with each other. They may even enjoy copying one another's efforts and ideas. However, the moment one toddler takes a special liking to another's little shovel, he may just grab it for himself, quite unconcerned by the perplexed consternation or howling cry this produces in his companion. Moreover, when he is intent on getting out of the sandbox, he may think nothing of using his playmate's body as a stepping stone, and when his mother brings him a cookie he would not dream of sharing it, much less of going without for the sake of pleasing his "friend." Insofar as babies or toddlers render services for others (even their mothers) or give to them of their own belongings, they are not motivated by generosity or selfless concern. They either take pleasure in doing instead of being done to, such as putting their food or spoon into mother's mouth as she has done to them, or they part with their things because they happen not to want or need them at the time. Even very young preschoolers' social attitudes are still marked by parallel play, lack of true consideration, use of others for their own ends, minimal appreciation of the feelings of others and association by convenience (E. Furman, 1992b, 1993).

During the nursery school years, however, we see some prestages of the capacity for friendship: There are brief periods of give-and-take play ("I'll be the mommy and you'll be the child and then we'll take turns and you can be the mommy and I'll be the child"). There are incidents where one's ideas and wishes are compromised for the sake of continuing the desired joint activity ("We don't have to make a parking lot. Will you go on playing if we build your garage?"). A gift may be shared or given in order to gain a playmate's admiration or willing participation in an activity ("Come look at my new game. You can play it with me"; or, "You can have one of my candies and then we'll play firemen"). We see even true episodes of empathy and concern for others. ("Jimmy's crying for his mommy. There, you can hold my teddy, Jimmy") Such moments in the nursery school are as encouraged and praised as they are rare because, at this stage in their development, children still are more often focused on the exclusive one-to-one relationship with the parent or teacher. It is mainly for the sake of the loved adult that other children are tolerated or even liked. The bond with the adult gives rise both to feelings of rivalry with other children and to the wish to be nice to them and interact with them in as friendly a fashion as the beloved grown-up does (A. Freud, 1963).

In the preschool years we see also the beginnings of other forms of association between children which are sometimes mistaken for true friendship. Among these are associations sought and maintained for self-aggrandizement, for status, for acceptance and for relief of feelings of inadequacy. For example, a child may follow another, perform services for him, share his possessions with him, and say nice things to him in order to gain his good will and thereby share in his real or assumed admired qualities, and the "admired" partner may return favors because having admirers and being in demand enhance his self-importance. This self-serving one-sided or mutual arrangement between star and fan is not a friendship.

Another type of early association is that of being accomplices in wrongdoing, which has the advantage of shared guilt seeming like half the guilt, and it indeed binds people to each other, but is not a tie of friendship. Young children sometimes accept or seek out partners-in-trouble. When "we" spill the paints or snitch the cookies, it does not feel half as bad as when "I" do it and, when apprehended by the authorities that be, "we" feel more powerful and less threatened by them than "I" alone. A related form of pseudofriendship is the association based on shared sexual interests. For example, children may team up to "play doctor" which is sometimes a euphemism for investigating each other's bodies or engaging in mutual sexual manipulations. Or children's excitement may be expressed less directly in high-pitched chasing, tumbling, and fighting which, as the adults usually predict, tends to end in somebody's tears or in damage to property.

Of course, such associations are not limited to preschoolers. They are common at all stages of growing up and persist even with some adults, but are always indicative of emotional immaturity and/or inability to cope adequately with inner conflicts and impulses.

This does not mean, however, that a real friendship excludes any other form of relationship between people. For example, a teacher or parent can also be a friend, especially in later years, and a husband and wife may be friends as well as sexual partners. Similarly, two young children may at times be companions in trouble or in excitement or serve to enhance each other's self-esteem, but at other times they may interact as real friends. It is a matter of degree as to which relationship predominates.

A real, sustained capacity for friendship develops toward the end of the preschool years and during the first years of elementary school. It is a period when boys and girls have grown to be loving and thoughtful in their relationships with their parents, and have aspired to achieve an exclusive mutually satisfying bond with one or the other parent. They will have eventually resigned themselves to the inevitable disappointment that such an exclusive bond is not possible because a parent–child relationship cannot also be a husband–wife and father–mother relationship. When children are in the process of coming to this realization we often see it reflected in their relationships with peers. We may, for example, see a touchingly attentive and considerate attempt to "woo" another child and to establish a loving boy–girl relationship. The pair may act like mature friends but the undertones of a hopeful erotic tie show themselves in the occasional earnest statement: "When I grow up I'll marry her (or him)." Or we may see children who are always intent on having an exclusive "friend," but the main purpose of it is to exclude a third party: "*We* won't play with *him*, will we?" Here the frustration and anger at the home situation, where the parental twosome feels like a rejection, shows itself in the child's turning the tables on an innocent peer: "He is left out, not I."

When the inner acceptance of one's status in the family has taken place, it becomes possible for the child to sense that other children are in the same boat, that they find themselves in the same circumstances and suffer the same hardship. This common bond of experiencing the same feelings enables the child to empathize and sympathize with his peer, to extend to him the thoughtful consideration learned in the relationship with the parents, to accept the other child's proffered kindness and comfort, and to enjoy the shared togetherness. And thus friendships come to be.

Nobody ever has many friends, and even the best friendships may end as personalities and circumstances change. A great deal may depend on the capacity of both partners to surmount obstacles, to forgive shortcomings, to tolerate disappointments and differences. No friendship, however, can flourish unless the foundation has been laid in the context of the late preschooler's relationship with his parents and his ability to come to terms with the limitations inherent in it. There are people who do not fully achieve the level of a giving, considerate relationship to their parents or who do not master the necessary disappointments it brings. They may remain at the prestages of friendship limited in nature and continuity, and/or their friendships may repeatedly end in frustration or disillusionment because they are invaded by other interests and motivations. Sometimes such complications are phase appropriate; for example, friendships among adolescents are readily affected by the young person's strong sexual and aggressive impulses or by his sense of inadequacy. In the former case a friendship may also become a sexual relationship or be interrupted for the sake of a sexual partner, or may turn into a partnership of accomplices in wrongdoing; in the latter case the need for acceptance or enhancement of self-esteem may determine the choice, or change of companion; for example, an adolescent may choose a "wrong" friend because he feels that no one "better" would accept him. At later periods in life, in adulthood, interferences in the ability to have a friend are usually a sign of personality difficulty.

**IF ONE HAS NOT GONE THROUGH THE
EXPERIENCE OF LOVING ONE'S PARENTS
AND OF ACCEPTING BEING LEFT OUT IN
SOME WAYS, CAN ONE STILL LEARN TO HAVE
FRIENDS LATER?**

Making friends is not learned in one day or even just at one time in one's life. Inner growth enables people to improve their friendships and to make them more lasting. At some periods in life friends may be more important than at other periods. At each phase of life, shared experiences and interests provide new opportunities and impetus for friendships, such as attending the same school, liking the same hobbies, working at the same job, serving together in the armed forces, living through a period of hardship, rearing a family at the same time. However, without experiencing an early give-and-take love with one's parents and without mastering its limitations, a child does not begin really to seek a friend and does not know how to give of himself to a friend.

DO FRIENDS INFLUENCE ONE'S CONSCIENCE?

That depends on the meaning of this question. If one means whether "friends can lead one astray," the answer would be, "Yes, they sometimes can lead one astray but that does not affect the nature of one's conscience." Allowing oneself to be led astray may be due to one's conscience tolerating whatever misdemeanor one is indulging in, or it may be due to one's conscience not serving as a reliable inner guide to behavior. In either case, those that have led one astray have not influenced one's conscience. We have either chosen to go along with them because their values and precepts are similar to our own or because we have not listened to our conscience. School children need much practice in learning to live with their consciences and to utilize them appropriately as an inner guide. Adolescents too sometimes experience trouble in this respect. When parents say, "Don't go out with so-and-so, he'll get you into trouble," they simply mean that they do not trust their child's conscience to help him resist temptation.

In another way, however, friends can influence one's conscience, in the sense that all long-term meaningful relationships
can add to or modify some aspects of our values, ideals, and
standards. The basic "parental" conscience always remains a
part of a person's conscience and additions or modifications are
most likely to be integrated when they are not too much at
variance with it. After all, our very wish and ability to maintain meaningful relationships with others and to take into
ourselves admired aspects of their personalities is part and
parcel of our early relationship with our parents and of the
conscience that grew out of it. Those who could not be influenced by their parents in such a way as to develop a conscience
cannot acquire a new or different one from others in later
phases of life. It may sometimes seem that our values are very
different from our parents' but, on closer inspection, we may
find, for instance, that our very ability to find individual solutions to life's problems is the principle we took over from them.
Perhaps they too chose to differ from their parents' precepts.

RELATIONSHIPS WITH SIBLINGS

Living in the same family and sharing the same parents constitute a special mutual bond between the children but does
not lead to a uniform or constant type of relationship between
them. Even a limited glance at any ordinary family quickly
reminds us that the relationships between siblings are complex, ever changing, and individually varied. The D. family may
serve as an example. Yvonne was the third child in the D. family and was barely two years old when a baby sister was born.
Yvonne was evidently fond of her eight-year-old brother Charlie.
He often helped his mother to take care of Yvonne, even baby-
sat with her for brief periods, readily let her play with some of
his toys, shared his candies, and played little games with her.
But since he spent most of his time with his own friends and
activities, Yvonne did not see very much of him, and even when
he was around, Yvonne often preferred to be with her mother
and did not like it at all when Mom and Charlie did something
together that meant she had to wait. In fact, she often protested
and interfered between them or interrupted them by getting

into trouble. Charlie, for his part, sometimes couldn't be bothered with Yvonne, could get quite cross with her, and complained when Mom couldn't do something for him because she had to take care of Yvonne.

Relations between Yvonne and four-year-old Jack were less smooth. Jack too occasionally "mothered" Yvonne but his attentions were less appropriate and thoughtful, and Yvonne was much less cooperative with him. Sometimes she teased him and wouldn't allow him to do things for her, sometimes he was too forceful and strict, so that their interactions often ended in struggles and cries for mother's immediate help. At times Jack and Yvonne played together contentedly for a while, usually with *her* toys, and she enjoyed his companionship and tried to copy his inventive ideas and superior skills. But these moments too tended to deteriorate. Either he became too bossy and she too frustrated, or he wouldn't allow her access to his toys and she grabbed back her own and destroyed what he had made. Again Mom's help was needed. Jack and Yvonne were also much more rivalrous of one another in regard to their parents, demanding more exclusive attention for themselves and resenting love, time, and energy spent on the other. It was a good thing that Yvonne's naptime freed Mom for Jack and his morning at the nursery school freed her for Yvonne. The times when Jack and Yvonne seemed least desirous of their parents and most satisfied with each other's company were the very times when Mom and Dad hurried to them most urgently. They knew that such quiet episodes indicated that Jack and Yvonne were partners-in-trouble and that they had to "Go see what the children are doing and tell them not to."

With her newborn sister Yvonne really did not yet have a relationship at all. She had shown clearly that she had not been in favor of Mom having another baby. She was both sad and angry at mother's care of little Janie. Although Yvonne sometimes watched the baby with interest and helped Mom by bringing clean diapers, Mom had to watch very closely to make sure that Yvonne's tentative gentle touching of Janie would not suddenly turn into a push or pinch. For the most part Yvonne's interest focused on preoccupying mother. Indeed, she seemed to need mother more than before Janie was born and was less willing to accept Charlie's or Jack's care.

The brothers were less perturbed by Janie's arrival. At times they resented Mother's attention to her but more often they were proudly helpful and disappointed that Janie paid as yet no heed to their attentive smiles and coos. Their interaction with one another sometimes included give-and-take play and sometimes rivalry, and sometimes they seemed to live apart in different worlds. But when they were not with their parents, as, for example, when playing with other children in the neighborhood, Charlie was often quite protective of Jack and the latter relied on his brother for help and comfort. Just recently they sometimes talked with each other seriously about other children, or TV programs, or football players.

At this time in the D. family the siblings' relationships were certainly far from simple or uniform. Janie was just beginning to form a relationship with her mother, and her brothers and sister would not play much of a part in her life for many months. Yvonne viewed Janie as a mere intruder into or rival for her relationship with her mother. The rivalry elements were also marked in her relationship with Jack, less so with Charlie. He was regarded mainly as a parent substitute or additional parental figure, whereas Jack was more of a playmate and perhaps partner-in-trouble. To Jack, Charlie was some of each—playmate, additional parent, rival—but there were also little beginnings of friendship. If we were to follow this particularly fortunate and loving family for some years in their development and on into adulthood, we would no doubt note many changes in their relationships. However, in the future as much as in the present, each child's level of personality development and individual circumstances would affect his or her view of the siblings.

The younger the child and the more exclusively he still needs the parents to maintain basic physical and mental well-being, the less welcome are brothers or sisters who are "new" or very close in age. No advantage is felt to derive from them; on the contrary, they are more likely experienced as a threat to oneself and as a sign of rebuff by the parents. It takes time and reassuring words and experiences for a young child to realize that the sibling is not an intolerable interference. It takes even more time and a loving relationship with the parents before the child can identify with the parents' love and care for all. As the young child increasingly wants to be like Mommy and Daddy and enjoys doing for someone else what has been done for him, it becomes possible to "be nice" and to "mother" or "parent" the little sibling.

Preschoolers as well as younger children tend to regard new siblings as a threat to be dealt with, as the following memories of young adults illustrate. "I am the oldest in our family and I was just over four when my first brother was born. After he'd been home for a week I helped my mom get the wastebaskets ready for the weekly garbage collection and I said to her, 'Let's put the baby out in the trash. He's been here long enough.' My mother said, 'No, we don't put babies in the trash. Bobby is going to be with us always and you'll see there'll be enough love for everyone.'"

"I was three-and-a-half when my mother had my younger sister. I remember one day a neighbor came to see the baby and I wouldn't leave my mom alone and kept hanging onto her and asking for things. Then the neighbor lady said, 'Your mommy has a baby now so she won't have time for you.' But my mom hugged me and said, 'That's ridiculous.' My mother told me that soon I began to try to amuse my little sister by dragging her around on a blanket and now we're great friends."

When children learn to like and care for their younger siblings in a parental way, the younger ones relate to them as additional, or substitute, parents, as we saw with Yvonne and Charlie and, to a lesser extent, with Yvonne and Jack. The children's feelings for and with their parents are, in this way, a great help to their relationship with each other even though it can bring some drawbacks; for example, the children may direct at one another feelings from their relationship with their parents that are less helpful to their interaction, such as anger, envy, or wishes for exclusive closeness.

The siblings' common bond with their parents as well as their joint experiences may increasingly promote other types of association among them—as playmates, as accomplices-in-trouble, or as mutual "boosts" for extra "power" vis-à-vis outsiders or even vis-à-vis the parents. For example, "*We* don't like stew" or "*We* don't want to go to bed" promises more impact on Mom than "*I* don't," especially when one worries a bit that being the only rebellious one may send one's share of Mom's love to the brother or sister who is "good." When the children reach the stage of being able to engage in friendship, siblings may become friends. They may empathize with each other's feelings and support one another or find comfort with each other at times when the parents have proved disappointing.

Usually, however, children form friendships first with peers outside the immediate family. There are several reasons for this. When siblings are very close in age, their rivalry for the parents' relationship tends to interfere. When there is a considerable age difference, they lack shared interests and the parent–child bond between them may overshadow their feeling of being in the same boat. Also, as they grow from one phase to another, their relative closeness changes; for example, an eight- and ten-year-old may feel they have much in common but three years later, as eleven- and thirteen-year-olds, the younger one is still apt to feel and act like an elementary school child, whereas the older one may consider himself a teenager. Also, the intensity of their togetherness and the intimacy of daily living, so similar to their feelings with the parents, introduces elements of conflict. As siblings grow older, as their age difference becomes less significant, as their emotional dependence on the parents lessens, and as their relationships outside the family become more meaningful, their chances of being friends increase.

WHY DO SIBLINGS SOMETIMES NEVER BECOME FRIENDS?

Many factors may contribute to this, some of which we have touched upon: for example, their age difference may be too great for the mutual feelings of parent–child to be overcome; their very closeness in age may accentuate and perpetuate their rivalry for the parents; their individual experiences within the family may differ so much that it may be difficult for them to empathize with each other (one sibling may suffer serious illnesses or separations from home, or may maintain a very different relationship with the parents, or may have very different individual gifts or deficits); being of the same or opposite sex may also play its part, sometimes facilitating a relationship and sometimes creating an interference; and a child's position in the family may, but need not, be a factor.

One of the most important and ever-present factors is the nature of the siblings' relationships with their parents. Sibling relationships are greatly helped when the parents are able to form a satisfactory relationship with each of their children and when they can help each child to express to them both his positive and negative feelings (anger, frustration, disappointment, competitiveness, jealousy, envy, etc.). When feelings toward the parents are deflected from their true targets and diverted to brothers or sisters, they cannot be appropriately mastered and tend to burden the relationships between siblings. For example, anger at the new baby is, to a considerable extent, anger that really belongs to the parents who are responsible for the baby's arrival; envy of the older brother's possessions and accomplishments is, to some extent, envy of the parents' even more superior attributes; jealousy of sister's friends may, likewise, become excessive when it also includes jealousy of the parents' love for each other and their exclusive relationship. It is not easy for parents, or anyone, to acknowledge to themselves that they cause hardship to their children and to accept the children's blame. Children, for their part, find it much easier to divert their "unacceptable" feelings from parents to siblings. In doing so they avoid antagonizing the parents ("You don't bite the hand that feeds you") and gain a ready opportunity for direct discharge (it is easier to hit or snatch something from a sibling). As a result parents and children are often inclined to take troubles between siblings at face value instead of viewing them as a sign of trouble between parents and children.

Sam and Bruce, aged eight and five, were always in trouble with each other when the parents went out together. Bruce would interfere with Sam's activities and Sam would belittle Bruce, often to the point of loud arguments and fist fights. Their irritability with each other would continue throughout the evening and, on their return or the next day, the parents often had to help resolve the boys' quarrels and accusations of one another. The parents eventually realized that their sons' hard feelings for one another at these times really related to their unhappiness about the parents' outing. They shared this idea with the boys and suggested they could tell Mom and Dad when they didn't like being left, or felt left out of a nice time, instead of taking it out on each other. As Sam and Bruce, with reminders, began to complain directly to their parents ("Yah, you always get to go out"; "I wish I could stay up late. It isn't fair"), they had less trouble with each other and could often support each other in a friendly way.

DOES IT HELP ONE TO MAKE FRIENDS IF ONE HAS BROTHERS AND SISTERS OR ATTENDS A NURSERY SCHOOL?

Living with other children inside and outside the family helps one to get to know what others are like, how they are similar or different, and which are their good and bad qualities. With the help of parents and nursery school teachers, children also learn the necessary social rules of interacting with one another: how to ask someone to play with you, how to take turns, how to offer and accept ideas, how to settle quarrels. These are very important aids in choosing a friend and in getting along with him but they do not produce friendship. The crucial factor is the child's experiences in his relationships with his parents and teachers which lead to his wish to like others as the loved adults do and to have a caring partnership.

An only child without access to peers may lack opportunity to make friends or may lag in the know-how of interacting with others, but he would still develop the wish and capacity for friendship through his relationship with his parents, and this would prompt him to long for a friend and to seek one.

ARE TWINS' RELATIONSHIPS DIFFERENT FROM OTHER SIBLING RELATIONSHIPS AND ARE TWINS MORE LIKELY TO BE FRIENDS?

The personality development of twins poses a special task for the parent–child relationship. It is difficult, but not impossible, for a mother to invest herself equally and at the same time in two babies and to meet their simultaneous demands in such a way that each child can develop a fully differentiated independent personality. Insofar as the parents succeed in this task, identical as well as fraternal twins' rivalry may be exaggerated but their eventual chances for becoming friends may also be enhanced. The danger lies in parents not relating to each twin fully and individually. This may cause inadequate personality development in one or both twins and impairment in their functioning as independent individuals. When twins unduly depend on each other it may not be a sign of friendship but an indication of insufficient self-differentiation or unresolved rivalry (Burlingham, 1952; Burlingham and Barron, 1963).

RELATIONSHIPS WITH GRANDPARENTS

Societies assign different roles to grandparents. In North American and European countries the grandparents' function varies considerably from group to group, from family to family. In some cases, the grandparents carry the main parental authority. Their wishes and decisions are binding on their adult children and may significantly affect the handling of the grandchildren. Other groups conceive of the ideal grandparent as an ever-available, yet never intruding, additional parent, who is a little less strict and more tolerant than the parent, who supports the child a bit against the parent, and somewhat softens the parent's authority, but who never interferes in the parent–child relationship.

Be their role that of additional parent, substitute parent, or "superparent," the grandchild may look to them for comfort and support when he is a bit at odds with his parents, or needs some respite from them, or when he simply enjoys the satisfactions of an additional and different relationship. This may, in a helpful way, enrich the child's experience and lessen his total dependence on the parents. In practice it is rare for all four grandparents to be alive and available. They may be ill or live far away. Moreover, grandparents may be unable to maintain appropriate relationships with their children and grandchildren. They may be intolerant and critical of the parents' parental functioning, causing resentments and loyalty conflicts between the generations; they may be so demanding of their children's care and attention that they become the grandchild's rival; or they may be disinclined to participate in any way in the lives of their children and grandchildren.

Yet, regardless of individual circumstances, grandparents still play a special part in the grandchildren's lives, and relationships with them are eagerly sought as soon as children are developmentally ready for relationships beyond the basic parent–child bonds. The parents' close relationship with the grandparents forms an important link. As is the case with mother's fondness for father, and with both parents' fondness for the other siblings, children want to get to know and love those who share in the parents' affection. But the parents' parents are important also in another way. They represent the continuity of the changing generations, the proof that parents were once children and that children grow up to be parents. They afford a look into the past (it is comforting to know that parents were not always powerful and perfect) and a look into the future (there is room in the world for parents and children when one grows up). Children rarely tire of hearing grandparents' stories of their parents' childhood, especially if they include some of the parents' early shortcomings, and they are always glad to know that their parents will become grandparents in time, because sometimes it feels to little children that their own growing up may leave no place for their parents.

All this is especially significant and welcome for the preschooler who struggles with finding his place in the family and in the order of things, and who tries to come to terms with what he is now, whence he came, and whither he is going in life. At later phases in their development, and under specially fortunate circumstances, grandchildren and grandparents may even develop a relationship that comes close to friendship.

DO CHILDREN MISS GRANDPARENTS WHEN THEY HAVE NEVER HAD ANY?

Yes. When children, usually as preschoolers, become interested in growing up and learn that their parents were once little, they inquire into who took care of them. This brings the wish to get to know the grandparents, the joy in finding that one has a special tie with them as grandparents, or the disappointment that one does not. Many youngsters spontaneously seek out other older people when their grandparents are dead or absent. They may take a special liking to other relatives of the grandparents' generation, to elderly neighbors or friends of the family. Many families have such unofficial "adopted" grandparents who fill the important links between the generations.

7

The Teacher–Pupil Relationship

Up until now we have looked at the development of the infant's first, crucial, and all-inclusive relationship with the mothering person, at the growing child's increasing ability to form additional and different relationships with the father and other members of the family, and at the later beginnings of friendships which usually extend into the wider community. All these relationships are based on powerful mutual emotional bonds: they embrace all of the loved person—looks, actions, thoughts, likes, and dislikes. They provide many satisfactions—immediate bodily pleasures intermingled with more sophisticated joint interests and activities: there is hugging and kissing, giving and receiving of affection, togetherness around eating and around sleeping in the same home (what a treat it is to spend the night at Grandma's or at a friend's house!), caring and being cared for at times of need. There are shared hobbies, games, sports, learning things from and about each other, discussing matters of joint interest. Another hallmark of all these relationships is their continuity. Once established, we expect them to last, day in, day out, year after year. They endure and adapt to many changes in the partners and in the circumstances of their lives. When a family relationship or close friendship is interrupted (through death, separation, conflict, or withdrawal), we consider it a major distress, regardless of how old we may be.

TASK-ORIENTED RELATIONSHIPS

Let us now look at a kind of relationship which is so different that it may appear strange at first sight: its main focus is an activity or task which the partners jointly pursue. Their relationship revolves around it. They do not share other parts of their lives and may know little about them. They work toward a common goal, and, in contributing their share toward achieving it, they are more likely to look in the same direction rather than at one another. Their relationship provides only mental rewards and excludes bodily contact and gratifications. It is limited in time, in the sense that the partners only meet for agreed, relatively brief periods of the day or week, and in the sense that they expect the relationship to terminate after a period of months or years. And when the anticipated end does come, they expect it to cause minor, not major, distress. In spite of its special characteristics and limitations, this kind of relationship may be deeply felt and very meaningful. At times it may even be preferred to the intensely emotional family relationships, or may provide a welcome respite from them, because of its relative ease and calm.

Who maintains these very different task-oriented relationships? As adults we often enjoy several of them—with colleagues in our job or profession, with co-workers on various projects, or with men and women with whom we regularly get together to pursue a hobby. In childhood, the first such relationship usually is the teacher–pupil relationship. Even a brief look confirms that all the essential elements we listed apply to that relationship. The child entering elementary school and the teacher who welcomes him into the classroom accept the fact that they will spend a certain number of hours together five times weekly (i.e., they expect to meet only at specified times). The child wants to learn to read and the teacher is eager to help him do it; that is their common goal. Both feel that reading is a desirable and perhaps enjoyable skill, worth a lot of hard work to achieve, and each pitches in: the teacher with lesson plans, board work, teaching aids, worksheets; the child with concentrated attention, with laborious sounding out of letters and words, and with pencil tightly grasped to reproduce the difficult shapes. Both partners take it for granted that each has to contribute his or her share to the joint work in pursuit of their goal, and neither finds it easy going. Each has to face mistakes, frustrations, and setbacks. Patience sometimes threatens to run out. But together they experience the thrill of the first word recognized or sounded out, of the worksheet correctly completed, of the primer read aloud haltingly, of the news "I read a word in my dad's newspaper." These shared pleasures cement their liking for one another, as do the hard times when the teacher's encouraging word helps the pupil to overcome a sense of failure, or when the child's appreciative, "Gee, I *like* that worksheet" lifts the teacher's spirits on a hard day. They build their relationship through their joint work and derive their satisfactions from it as well as from the hard-won piecemeal successes which bring them closer to their goal.

Yes, it all sounds very austere. Yet, for many of us, this relationship, tied to the first pains and pleasures of learning to read, is so important and so deeply felt that our elementary school teacher forever retains a special, fond place in our hearts, even if we never see him or her again in later years. It was, after all, a relationship discontinued as planned after a certain time.

There are, however, also many among us who do not treasure these early experiences. Learning with a teacher may have never brought satisfaction or success, only boredom, or shame and failure, or an unbearable sense of a chore from which we could not wait to escape. In some instances all this changed for the better in later years, or felt better with some teachers or with some subjects, or outside a school setting, such as in a job or in extracurricular activities. With others all learning may have remained unhappy, and such people avoid being a pupil at all cost.

We often blame unsatisfactory learning experiences on poor teachers, lazy pupils, lack of adequate equipment, or uninterested parents, and we suggest and try many remedies. Perhaps teachers should be nicer, or more demanding, or more punitive; learning should be made exciting with the help of games, or more rewarding with the help of candies or prizes; or it should focus more on the basics, or be enforced with structure and discipline; parents should be involved in the school and with the child's homework, or they should stay out of the way altogether and leave the child's schooling in the hands of the teacher.

It is rarely recognized that learning depends primarily on a true teacher–pupil relationship. It is even more rarely appreciated what this kind of relationship is about, what each partner has to contribute, and when and how a child develops the capacity to engage effectively in such a relationship. So let us now think about all this and what it entails.

THE CHILD'S READINESS TO FORM A RELATIONSHIP WITH A TEACHER

Three- or three-and-a-half-year-olds are usually ready to take the difficult developmental step of entering a nursery school. During their few hours of regular attendance there they learn to form the beginnings of a teacher–pupil relationship. How do we know when this is accomplished? Many signs tell us: The child is eager to go to nursery school, comfortable in leaving mother and in functioning at school without her, yet glad to welcome her at the end of the session, and ready to return home. He differentiates parent from teacher, home from school, and accepts certain differences between them—differences in rules, in behavioral expectations, in the type of activities and available materials, and in traditions, such as how holidays are celebrated. The child is also able to bridge the gap between home and school, perhaps by sharing with the parents what happened at school (he does not expect them just to know without having to be told). He shares with the teacher what happens at home in appropriate ways (an account of an outing, a new toy to show and share, a feather for the science corner) rather than inappropriately (a garbled story of his night fear, a baby blanket, an object from home which nobody should touch). His fondness for the teacher shows in eagerness to join in the activities she offers, in enjoyment of the materials she provides, and in efforts at mastering the skills she demonstrates. The child admires the teacher's know-how, accepts her suggestions, welcomes her encouragement and praise, but also takes pride in his own work and achievements. The child rarely gives or expects physical affection or demands bodily care, is independent in toileting, eating, and dressing for outside play or for going home. He may enjoy a snack at school, may solicit the teacher's help with a hard zipper, may allow her to put a Band-Aid on a scratch, but does not consider these services her main function, and takes it for granted that the teacher attends to all the children. Sharing her love and attention with them is no special hardship.

In all these ways the child often behaves "better" at school than at home, a fact that mothers and teachers sometimes erroneously attribute to the teacher's better educational methods. Actually, the difference in the child's behavior stems from the difference in the nature of the relationship. The longstanding, intense emotional closeness between mother and child makes for more conflict in their interaction but it also paves the way for the child's ability to relate to a teacher and to behave like a pupil. No child is capable of these advanced achievements without having experienced, and benefited from, a great deal of good mothering.

The mother's part starts years before entry to nursery school. As we know, her continuous caring relationship with her baby enables him to grow into a person in his own right in the first place and, gradually, to develop skills and interests which make it possible and enjoyable for him to be more independent and to relate to others on new terms. In order to be ready to form a teacher–pupil relationship and to contribute his share to its joint task, the child must have mastered many steps with the help of his relationship with the mothering person. Let us list these steps in personality growth and group them under a few headings:

1. *Taking Care of Many of His Own Bodily Needs:* self-feeding, dressing, control of elimination, and ability to avoid common dangers, such as electric outlets and hot stoves. As long as the child depends on a mothering person to meet these basic bodily needs, he cannot be comfortable without her. Such children either require the mother's presence in addition to the teacher or they relate to the teacher as a mother substitute.

2. *Mastering His Urges and Feelings to a Considerable Extent:* being able to wait, to accept substitute gratifications, to use words for needs, feelings, and thoughts and to communicate them to others, to tolerate some disappointment or failure. Babies and toddlers want what they want, now, be it getting their dinner, reaching for their teddies, seeing their

moms, building a block tower, or using a hammer. The urge is so strong and immediate that the infant cannot postpone it, or give it up, or do something else instead. Very young children pursue their wishes with all the verve they can muster, and if something proves unattainable they tend to become overwhelmed with rage and despair. It's a long way to being a youngster who is sufficiently master of himself to learn with a teacher in a classroom!

3. *Achieving a Measure of Consideration for Others:* so that one's anger at them will be tempered and sufficiently restrained to safeguard them and the relationships with them. When we remind ourselves of the toddler's unmitigated outbursts of temper, of his "bearhug" mixture of affection and destruction, and of his actual disregard for his peers, we realize how far he is from being able to participate in cooperative work and social interaction.

4. *Enjoying Activities That Involve a Measure of Effort and Skill and Aim Toward Achievement:* such as building with blocks or making sandpies. For a long time youngsters can appreciate and sustain such activities only for very limited periods. The sandpies soon deteriorate into mud baths and the blocks are knocked down or thrown around.

5. *Building Relationships Around Companionship and Shared Activities in Which the Loved One, at Least at Times, Is Not Regarded as a Mother Substitute:* these relationships, usually with family members, still include bodily closeness and an all-embracing emotional interest in one another, but they are a stepping stone toward the later teacher–pupil relationship, with its specific purpose of learning in the narrower goal-directed sense.

How do youngsters accomplish all that? Slowly. Parental help in all these areas starts early on and continues all along. Learning to relate to a teacher and to contribute appropriately to that relationship is by no means easy, even when children have maintained a good relationship with the mothering person (E. Furman, 1969a, 1977a, 1977b, 1992b, 1993; R. A. Furman and A. Katan, 1969).

Preschoolers and some young elementary school children are apt to view the teacher initially as a mother-substitute or family member. This may show in inappropriate expectations of the school (always wanting to sit by the teacher, hold her hand on walks, or kiss and be kissed) or in a loyalty conflict between mother and teacher (teasing mom with "I like Mrs. A. better" or worrying whether one likes the teacher better than mother). Children also sometimes lag in self-care (expecting the teacher to help with toileting, with dressing, or with wiping runny noses). They are not always masters of their urges and feelings (fidgeting during stories, running around the room at snacktime, grabbing materials from others, refusing to compromise on using crayons when their heart is set on painting just then, sitting forlornly in a corner instead of telling the teacher of a tummy ache or of a hurt inflicted by another child). Anger is occasionally still expressed in loud yells, punches, or destruction of materials when the teacher's rules feel too annoying, when another child gets a first turn at the new game, or when the child's frustration at not being able to make the scissors cut outreaches the limits of his tolerance. Immediate bodily pleasures are sometimes still preferred to the hard-to-achieve taste of success with skills, as when the paint is gleefully smeared over table, child, and floor instead of being laboriously worked into a picture, when the blocks are made to crash loudly instead of being used to construct a building, or when a baseball practice deteriorates into an angry–excited free-for-all. In short, at the start of nursery school and even at the start of elementary school, the young child is still learning to be a pupil, learning to make his contribution to the joint task, and learning to appreciate the teacher's role (E. Furman, 1994b).

THE ROLE OF THE TEACHER

But what is the teacher's role? That is simple to state but difficult to appreciate fully, even for teachers. It consists of liking the subject or skill one teaches, and of wanting to learn ever more about it. It also consists of liking the process of teaching and learning, and of supporting and enjoying the pupil's learning. Last but not least, it includes deriving satisfaction from the pupil's work and from the successes he achieves. These contributions by the teacher are as crucial to teaching how to cut with scissors or build with blocks as they are to teaching reading and arithmetic, or astronomy and history, or child development.

Let us take a closer look at what these statements imply. Is it really important for a teacher to like his subject? Is it even possible for him to like it and to want to learn ever more about it? How can one like counting to 100, or simple addition, or printing letters? How can one go on liking such things year after year? Yes, one can like these activities and one can continue to like them. Every good kindergarten teacher indeed does like them, just as every good nursery school teacher likes building with blocks and playing beginners' board games, and collecting leaves or acorns, and just as every good mother enjoys bathing and dressing her child. There is no skill too humble to like, too unimportant to merit interest, or too simple to execute well without dedicated effort. And those who choose to teach it need to consider it worthwhile, need to like and respect it. Unless they do, they cannot derive satisfaction from their work, nor can they convey their positive interest to the pupil. One of the reasons children sometimes don't like to do household chores is that they are asked to do the chores the parents don't like to perform, but when the parents do enjoy a chore (yes, many mothers enjoy doing dishes and folding laundry!) the children are eager to learn it with them and to take it over.

As for liking the process of teaching and learning, is it really true that a teacher has to like both? Is it not enough to like the teaching part of it? Is it not the whole point of being the teacher that one is the one who knows all about it? No, it is not. Teachers who only like to teach cannot want to learn more about their subject or more about the methods of teaching it. They cannot empathize with their pupils or learn from them. Pupils teach the teacher a great deal about his subject as well as about how it is learned and how it is best taught. Above all, a teacher who does not enjoy learning can never help a pupil experience pleasure in learning. He can, at best, make him feel that it is superior fun to teach and inferior misery to learn.

What does it mean "to support and enjoy the pupil's learning"? Learning is an arduous task which requires many skills, some general (like concentration and frustration tolerance) and some specific (like small muscle control for writing or ability to think with symbols for doing arithmetic). Each skill has to be learned, applied appropriately, and perfected. This makes up the process of learning. A teacher who does not appreciate all aspects of this process and does not support and enjoy its unfolding and development in the pupil misses out on much of what teaching and learning are all about. Getting there is half the fun. A baseball player who only likes to win and has neither interest nor enjoyment in the technical intricacies and skills of the game is not a truly dedicated sportsman. Similarly, the good teacher not only wants his students to achieve well but is interested in how they learn, assists them with the learning process, and appreciates their struggles.

The results, however, are important too. Here we come to the teacher "deriving satisfaction from the pupil's work and from the successes he achieves." A teacher can and should be pleased with his contribution to the joint task, but he must be clear in himself that the goal is the pupil's acquisition of knowledge for himself. Insofar as this goal is reached, the success belongs to the pupil. The knowledge or skill the pupil has gained by dint of his own efforts, and with the teacher's help, is his to use, to enlarge, or to set aside and forget as he wishes. It is also his to enjoy. The teacher can share in it only by enjoying the fact that the pupil is pleased with his achievement. This implies that the teacher enjoys the pupil becoming more of an equal or even surpassing him—a pleasure similar to that of the parent who enjoys seeing his child grow up without having to claim the child's success for himself or having to compete with him.

Whenever a teacher usurps the results of the joint work, the teacher–pupil relationship becomes distorted and ultimately affects the pupil's chances for wanting to learn for himself. Such distortions can take many forms; for example, assignments may be treated as a task the student performs for the teacher rather than to further his learning. ("*I* am very pleased that you handed in a correct worksheet" instead of "You did a fine job with your worksheet. I hope you are pleased with it") Time and effort expended on learning may be viewed as a way to satisfy the teacher rather than to satisfy the student. ("I like children who work hard" instead of "You'll really get good at that when you work so hard at it. That'll make you feel very good about yourself") A good grade may be given as a reward for producing what the teacher demanded rather than as a measure of the extent of knowledge or skill the student has acquired ("If you are a good boy and do everything I told you to, I'll give you an A," instead of "If you work hard at it you will achieve at A level"). The words themselves do not matter but the attitude they convey counts.

Of course, all this applies to the student's failure as much as to his success. The failures and dissatisfaction are the student's too. The teacher can sympathize with the pupil's unhappiness with himself, he can help him plan how to improve his work, or he may question the student's lack of seeming concern, but a pupil's failure should not be regarded as an insult or injury to the teacher, nor should it be countered with threats and punishment.

Does this mean that pupils should never be praised or receive awards for their legitimate achievements? Not at all. Everyone likes to be appreciated and receive recognition, and everyone sometimes likes a little deserved respite from hard work. By the same token, teachers need to feel and express dissatisfaction when the pupil's contribution to the joint work is inadequate or when he loses sight of the goal. But these are not the main incentives for learning.

Learning and achieving have to be one's own thing. They have to provide their own satisfactions and make us feel good about ourselves, otherwise we will not continue to learn when the external rewards or punishments cease or when we do not like the teacher. Above all, we would not enjoy learning itself, would not like what we learn or develop a lasting interest in it. The role of the teacher–pupil relationship does not include inducing the pupil to learn out of love for the teacher or out of fear of his disapproval, nor in order to be loved or to avoid punishment, nor in order to gain rewards which have nothing to do with learning, such as candies, free time, or parties. The teacher–pupil relationship does contribute an important part to the pupil's *wish* to learn, but that works in different ways.

Now we have come to the most important driving force in learning, the pupil's wish to learn. Even when pupil and teacher are able to contribute appropriately, they cannot successfully work together unless the pupil wants to learn, unless he is "motivated." Where does this wish to learn come from?

THE WISH TO LEARN

As with all developmental steps, the wish to learn comes neither automatically nor suddenly. Personality development resembles the growth of a plant in many ways. Just as the inherent potential of the seed is released by the available sun, water, and nutrients, so the development of the child's personality is shaped by the mutual interdependence between his maturational potential and his emotional and educational environment. With the wish to learn, as with every other stride, the environment—and especially the child's relationship with the parents and, later on, teachers—facilitates the unfolding of his endowment and helps bring it to fruition.

When we talked about the mother's relationship with her baby and toddler we saw that her role of meeting the child's needs and ministering to his body is gradually taken over by the child himself. The more consistent and satisfying the mother's care has been, the sooner does the child become a person in his own right and the sooner too does he signal, and often insist, that he wants to do for himself the very things mother had done for him. In the second half of the first year, we usually see one of the first steps in this direction—the baby grabs for the food, takes hold of the spoon or cup, and wants to be the one who does the feeding. When he is present at the family meal he may impatiently sideswipe his little dishes and clamor for bits from the parents' plates. Given a chance, he not only tries to feed himself but often tries to feed mother and his teddy or dolls. "Me do, me do, all by myself" is the healthy toddler's constant refrain. He pushes mother away and wants to dress himself, wants to reach his own cookies, wants to walk rather than be carried. Within months he also wants to become clean like his parents and learns to use the toilet as they do. In all these activities the child's wish to learn and do as his mother and father do stems primarily from his love and admiration for them, which prompt the drive to become like them.

We have already talked about this role of the parent–child relationship with the preschooler. There we saw how the love and admiration of the parents as a man and woman inspire the child's wish to be big, to look and do as they do. And we also talked about how the child comes to appreciate that he cannot be and do just like the grown-ups right away and re-signs himself to work toward that goal slowly, by learning their skills and by acquiring their knowledge for himself. The most desirable parental attributes and activities are usually those which the parents appear to value most in themselves and which seem to contribute most to their status in the child's view.

In this way the parent–child relationship fosters the child's wish to learn to become like the parents and provides a special incentive for him to learn what the parents like and enjoy. This is especially true when the parents offer the child an opportunity to learn and support his efforts. After the child has really mastered a new activity it gradually ceases to be "Something I can do like my dad" and becomes a part of the child himself, a part he enjoys, is proud of. It enhances his self-esteem.

Let us take reading as an example. John, a preschooler, observes closely all his beloved dad does. He notices that Dad likes to read the newspaper when he comes home in the evening. John knows a bit about what reading means be-cause now and then Dad reads out a paragraph to share with Mom or he tells her about what he has read. Now and then too, Dad or Mom reads a book to John. John handles the book, looks at the pictures, picks up the newspaper, and can't make sense out of it. He may feel something like "I wish I could read like Dad. I'd really fancy myself if I could read!" Next we find John pretending to read, turning the pages, and perhaps repeating phrases from a favorite story or jabber-ing away big nonsense words the way Dad sounds when he talks in big words to Mom. John feels great when he pretends to read like Dad, but after a while this good feeling gives way to one of disappointment or inadequacy when something or someone reminds him that he is not really reading like Dad. Mom and Dad probably notice John's wish to read. Perhaps they print out his name on a piece of paper by way of helping him to recognize this most important word, or they may show him letters in an alphabet book. Perhaps they just smile at him indulgently. Sooner or later, they are likely to say, "You'll have a chance to learn to read when you go to school. That's what school is for and there will be a teacher to help you." They offer him a realistic setting in which he can fulfill his wish to learn to read—in school, with a teacher. When learning eventually gets under way, John finds it slow and arduous but every letter and word mastered bring the glowing inner feeling, "Now I am closer to being really like Dad." This powerful motivation helps him to bear many frustrations. In time, reading gets to be enjoyable in its own right. It becomes John's own thing, not just a vehicle to becoming like Dad. He gets satisfaction from his achievement, from the new world books open up for him, and from his independence in being able to explore this world without having to beg or wait for others to read to him. He may then feel something like "I like reading and I like myself when I read. It feels good." If and when John comes to that point, we say that he has identified himself with his parent in regard to reading. Reading is now a part of him. He gains satisfaction from it and it helps him to be a more adult member of his family and community (E. Furman, 1994b).

The young child's wish to learn skills and to advance himself to more grown-up status stems primarily from his relationship with his parents, but this wish may not always include knowing how to read; for example, one kindergartner I knew showed no interest in reading. He was thought to have a learning problem until the teacher realized that the boy's father was illiterate, a fact the family kept secret. The boy's attitude changed markedly after the father acknowledged his illiteracy to his son, told him that he had not had a chance to learn but hoped very much that his boy would read and surpass him in this respect. Even in instances where the father takes pleasure in reading, however, the child's wish to emulate him depends on the nature of their relationship and on the father's support for his son's growing up.

Already early on, and increasingly so during the child's growing up, relationships with teachers (not necessarily in a school setting) serve a similar role of inspiring the wish to learn.

Within the framework of these relationships it is no longer the loved person's grown-upness which is admired, but his or her mastery and love of a particular subject. When a teacher really enjoys, say, science, is good at it, and finds it fascinating to study, and when he is also willing to share his knowledge with us and to help us enjoy it too, we often want to make his interest our own. We may feel, "Gee, I never knew bugs could be so interesting. I wish I knew more about them too. I'm going to get to work on that." Our new wish to learn about bugs may only last long enough to give us a glimpse of the new vista the teacher opened for us, or it may develop into a lasting hobby or even career. In either case, our new knowledge and skill is viewed as an end in itself; it enriches our lives. It is not, as with the very young child, a means of acquiring adult status (E. Furman, 1969b, 1985b, 1992b, 1993).

Sometimes even very little children are motivated to learn something as an end in itself when the offered or available activity brings special satisfactions; for example, many preschoolers want to learn to use scissors and thoroughly enjoy cutting out shapes; many love to draw or to work with clay. Now, they may have admired these activities when performed by a parent, teacher, or older sibling, and they may have gotten help from them in learning how to go about it, but they enjoy working at it for the fun and satisfaction it brings them. Their absorption, genuine pleasure in the process, and persistent effort at creating new, better, and different products all tell us that they are engaged in doing their own thing for its own sake, that the process of learning gratifies so much as to be a motivating force. There are other, much older children and even adults who are not interested in what they learn and do not get satisfaction from the process of learning, yet they do want to learn because they see it as a stepping-stone toward some desired end or achievement; for example, to achieve a high school diploma or college degree we may need to take courses we would not choose in order to accumulate enough credits. With this kind of motivation learning becomes much more of a chore, and we can hardly wait to get it over with and to enjoy the end result. Of course, learning is most enjoyable when the process as well as the goal is satisfying.

THERE MUST BE MANY PEOPLE WHO NEVER
FORM A RELATIONSHIP WITH A TEACHER
AND NEVER ENJOY LEARNING IN THAT WAY

We have described a perfect teacher–pupil relationship. In real life nothing is perfect and indeed should not be. All teachers, parents, and pupils make mistakes and get "off the track" at times. They also tend to overlap their relationships somewhat, so that elements from one extend into the other. A father is sometimes also a sitter, a teacher acts on occasion a bit like a mother-substitute or family member, and children, especially young children, inevitably cast them all into mixed roles now and then. Often enough, this enhances rather than interferes with the specific relationship between the partners; for example, a school party on special occasions is not strictly speaking a function of the teacher–pupil relationship but can serve to cement it through a friendly good time enjoyed together. Difficulty only arises when the essential aspects of the teacher–pupil relationship are not predominant: for example, when teacher and/or pupil altogether mistake the nature and purpose of their relationship (such as when the child treats the teacher as a mother who is there to take care of him and love him, or when the teacher treats the child as her offspring and mothers instead of teaching). Or they may misunderstand what teaching and learning are about, such as when they assume that it is like force-feeding or like a fight over who controls whom. Many people do maintain good enough, though not perfect, teacher–pupil relationships. They make mistakes, correct them, and learn from them.

There are, however, people who truly fail to form a relationship with a teacher. When this is due to a lag in their development, or due to a current stress in their lives, or due to an unhelpful teaching situation, they may well come into their own at a later time. If it is due to a difficulty within their own personality they may, in some instances, be able to overcome it with the help of psychological treatment. But some may indeed never be able to relate to a teacher as a teacher. Regardless of what may cause this, it still does not necessarily preclude all learning. Much can be learned even with the wrong methods and in far from ideal circumstances. Such learning, unfortunately, is often limited in one or another way. It may provide less satisfaction and add little to self-esteem. It may not be assimilated as a lasting part of our minds. It may not pave the way for a wish to learn more and may not prepare for later learning in higher grades, or may fail to serve as a means of adapting to a job in the community. It may be experienced as a waste of time and effort, and may even leave an aftertaste of bitterness.

DON'T MOST CHILDREN LEARN FOR THE "GOLD STAR" RATHER THAN FOR THEMSELVES?

It is nice to have both. Learning for oneself makes one independent, and brings a deeper, more lasting satisfaction, but it is quieter and less spectacular than the "gold star." This makes learning for oneself the easily forgotten pleasure. Many children, from early on, do actually enjoy learning but they are not always aware of it, especially when the adults stress the "star." Often children also prefer not to notice what they feel about their work because they are critical of it, more critical than the grown-ups. However, parents and teachers who recognize their own pleasure in learning and appreciate how great it is not to have to depend on others often help children to know their inner feelings, good and bad, and to value them.

When children appear not to look at their own work but right away rush it to the adult for praise and reward, they often do so to avoid self-appraisal. Perhaps in their own eyes their work would not be judged as favorably as in the eyes of the teacher or parent, and they therefore use the "Band-Aid" of adult acceptance to cover their own misgivings. When we ask children to assess their own work, we often hear an embarrassed "It's too sloppy," or "Jack's is better," or "These big letters are yucky" where we would have judged their efforts as very good. At such times we can help children to be less harsh with themselves, to better their self-esteem, and even to enjoy the "star" more, by talking over with them the discrepancy between their assessment and our own: "I think you are a bit too hard on yourself. To me your work looks better than to you. After all, you have only just begun to practice this and therefore I wouldn't expect it to be perfect. I think it's a very good first effort. In time it will get better yet." Praise which tallies with one's own assessment is much more appreciated than praise which substitutes for, or hides, self-criticism.

ARE THERE NOT MANY PEOPLE WHO LEARN ON THEIR OWN, PROMPTED BY THEIR SPECIAL GIFTS OR INTERESTS WHICH ARE DIFFERENT FROM THOSE OF THEIR PARENTS AND TEACHERS?

Superior intellectual or athletic endowment and innate artistic gifts do indeed provide motivation and gratification, and so do individual interests which, as we shall discuss later, are derived from the child's early bodily urges and feelings. However, none of these operate independently. The persistent, successful pursuit of an activity usually involves extra hard work and a good ability to learn from others. When Bach was praised for his genius, he is said to have replied, "Anyone who chooses to work as hard as I do, could produce the same or better music." We do not quite believe him but he does remind us that genius does not imply "it comes without effort and without learning," and both these attributes are closely related to upbringing.

Also, a person's gifts and special interests are usually affected by his or her relationships with parents and teachers; for example, loved adults may appreciate and support a child's activities without being good at them themselves. Some children identify with a parent's attitude; for example, the parent's interest in nature may help to develop his child's special interest in physics although the parent has no knowledge of physics in particular. Sometimes children take up interests just because they differ from the parents'; for example, a child's literary predilection may be related to the very fact that his parents have no interest in literature and present no competition to him in this field or will be unable to intrude upon his studies, but even such an indirect link with the parents is still significant as a motivating force. Moreover, teachers are not necessarily schoolteachers. A child's interest in drawing may stem from his relationship with a neighbor who "taught" him. There are also many early events, experienced with the parents, which stimulate special interests; for example, an interest in medicine or nursing may stem from experiences with illness and death in the family. Close and deep insight into an individual personality often reveals unsuspected links between specific activities and early relationships.

IF CHILDREN HAVE NOT HAD A SUFFICIENT ONE-TO-ONE RELATIONSHIP WITH THEIR MOTHERS, CAN THEY STILL BE HELPED TO HAVE A RELATIONSHIP WITH A TEACHER?

Unfortunately, it is not possible to build a second story onto a house which has no foundation or first floor. I think we would all agree that the first order of business would be to erect the missing substructure. Likewise, a child cannot start out with a teacher–pupil relationship. If a youngster has missed out on the necessary relationship with a mothering person, we would have to try and provide that first and hope that he could utilize it belatedly and make up for the earlier deprivation. The teaching situation, however, is not well suited to serve this end. Even a very kind, helpful, "motherly" teacher makes a poor mother-substitute. After all, what kind of mother is it who never shows up on weekends or vacations, who never cooks meals or cares for her child during sicknesses? These inevitable limitations interfere with a teacher's attempt at mothering and cause the child who regards the teacher as a mother too many disappointments and frustrations.

There are, however, some children who experienced some mothering but whose development has fallen a little short of reaching the stage of a teacher–pupil relationship. These children relate to a teacher as a partial mother-substitute and use the relationship to achieve some learning. Certain forms of individual tutoring and teaching in small groups with much individual attention are geared to help children with such difficulties.

AT WHAT POINT CAN A CHILD NO LONGER
MAKE UP FOR STEPS MISSED IN
HIS DEVELOPMENT?

We don't know a general answer because there are so many
individual variations—different children, different past experiences, different ways of making up. Many children have missed
out only on some aspects. Usually, the sooner a child can get
help and the more suited such help is to the child's specific
needs, the better are the chances of repairing early misfortunes.
Unfortunately, there are some who never get the right help or
for whom it comes too late.

IS IT NOT IMPORTANT FOR A TEACHER
TO LOVE CHILDREN MORE THAN TO LOVE
HIS SUBJECT?

In every community children are a minority group, perhaps the
most helpless and vulnerable of all minorities. Like other minority groups, and sometimes even more so, children are a
ready target for prejudice and as such are unrealistically loved
or hated, favored or mistreated. If a teacher's love of children
springs from such a prejudice, it is usually not helpful because
it has little to do with the qualities and needs of real individual
children and gets in the way of building appropriate relationships with them. In the same way, a teacher who hates or
detests children as a group cannot appreciate and relate to an
individual child sensibly.

   If, however, a teacher's love of children means that she
respects and treats each child as a person, is able to feel with
children and enjoy the give-and-take of relationships with them,
then we shall probably find that such a teacher likes some children more than others, depending on the teacher's and child's
particular personalities. It is not necessary to love one another
in order to get along and work together. It is necessary to be civil,
respectful, and appreciative of each other's contribution to the
joint undertaking. This applies to pupils, too. A child's successful learning does not necessarily depend on his like or dislike of
a particular teacher as a person. It tends to depend more on

the child's willingness and ability to apply himself and on the teacher's ability to convey her liking of the subject and to kindle the child's interest in it (E. Furman, 1990, 1992b, 1993).

HOW DOES THE TEACHER–PUPIL RELATIONSHIP CHANGE BEYOND ELEMENTARY SCHOOL?

There are some changes, but they happen only when the earlier relationships provided a good basis for further growth. The child's capacity for sustained work increases, as does the range of his interests and goals. Attitudes to learning and to the teacher which were still developing in the younger child and required much fostering become more firmly established: for example, learning for oneself, working toward one's own goals, understanding and accepting the teacher's role. Ultimately some people (and some children can even do this at times in elementary school) are able to learn without a "real" teacher. They may use books as a substitute or utilize experiences to teach them—observations, experiments. We sometimes even speak of life as a great teacher, but people can only learn from life if they know how to learn and want to be taught.

SHOULD NOT A TEACHER BE INTERESTED IN THE CHILD AS A WHOLE PERSON RATHER THAN CONCERN HIMSELF ONLY WITH THE CHILD'S LEARNING?

It depends on the nature of the interest and the reasons for it. The interest is appropriate if the teacher wants to know about all aspects of the child's personality in order to be able to help him better with his learning and to adapt the joint work and goals to the pupil's current capacities; for example, a child's chronic illness or temporary stress in the home may affect his learning and may require changes in teaching methods and goals.

The teacher's interest is less appropriate and helpful if its aim is to establish an all-encompassing, close emotional tie for its own sake or in order to help the child with those concerns which are not within the teacher's proper domain, such as unhappy relationships within the family or emotional problems. This could encourage the child to relate to the teacher as a family member or as a therapist and would then interfere with the teacher–pupil relationship and with the tasks it pursues. It is preferable to be a good teacher than a poor substitute for other people in the child's life. Often a teacher helps most by sympathizing with a child's distress and, if necessary, by alerting the parents or caregivers to his need.

IS IT NECESSARY FOR A CHILD TO GO TO A NURSERY SCHOOL TO LEARN HOW TO RELATE TO A TEACHER?

No, it is not essential. This developmental step can be taken at the start of elementary school. A good nursery school can be very helpful and facilitate entry to public school. A bad nursery school can be a harmful interference in the child's maturation.

8

Death and Bereavement

WHAT DOES "DEAD" MEAN? HOW DO CHILDREN LEARN ABOUT IT?

Most children encounter death earlier and more frequently than birth. As toddlers, sometimes as early as 18 months, sometimes a few months later, when they are usually able to distinguish animate from inanimate objects in their familiar surroundings, when they know that the teddy, doll, or table will not do things on their own whereas another child or animal will, they also observe that living functions can cease irrevocably, that what is alive can become dead. They note that the fly, swatted on the table, no longer buzzes, that the wasp sprayed with insecticide on the windowpane no longer flies around, that the ant or worm stepped on on the ground no longer crawls, that the squashed mosquito no longer stings. They do not expect them to resume their activities. They may pick up a dead insect or worm, finger it thoughtfully or squash it with glee, without concern that it may get away or that it may hurt them. They also know that these corpses are disposed of in certain ways, put into the garbage, flushed away, or thrown into the bushes. The occasional dead animal seen by the roadside and TV cartoons (often the first program toddlers watch) add to their experiences with death and emphasize deliberate or accidental killing as its cause. Death from natural causes, through old age or sickness, is most often encountered in relation to flowers and plants—the wilted bouquet, the leafless dead bush (E. Furman, 1990).

When parents allow themselves to be aware of their young-sters' observations, can listen to their spoken and implied ques-tions, and answer them realistically and calmly, they help them to form a competent basic concept of the concrete aspects of death. They then know that "dead" means the cessation of the living functions they can observe in themselves and in others: it does not move, eat, sleep; it does not make sounds, does not see, hear, or feel, not even pain. (Heartbeat, breathing, and brain activity are unfamiliar ideas for children and do not help them to understand death, but older toddlers sometimes add another function that is vital in their minds to the parent's list, "And it doesn't do BM.") They also know that "dead" means permanence, that a living thing can die but a dead one cannot regain life. They get to know some of the causes of death—purposeful and accidental hurt, sickness, and old age—and they learn quite a bit about the disposal of the dead, sometimes including burial, if a dead animal is buried in the backyard. They may even be familiar with some aspects of decomposition, such as the way it shows with plants (E. Furman, 1992b, 1993).

During the preschool years, experiences with death mul-tiply and afford many opportunities for the child to extend and deepen his concept of death. It may also become confused through new misunderstandings which need to be clarified, and through newly added feelings, some appropriate and some inappropriate, which have to be sorted out and coped with. Preschoolers inevitably see, hear, or overhear news items about deaths from TV, radio, newspaper pictures, and conversation. They watch television more often and are, at least peripher-ally, included in programs intended for older family members. In the city, they come across funeral processions and ambu-lances which hold up traffic, they drive by cemeteries and funeral homes; in rural areas, they are closer to experiences with hunting and fishing, with animals killing other animals, and with slaughter for food. Young children often contribute unwelcome inquiries to family meals: "Where did this meat come from?"; "Did they kill the cow?"; "Is the chicken dead now?"; "What part of the pig is this?"; "Did they hurt the pig and did it scream?" They also tend to comment freely on other reminders of death in daily life: "Is your fur coat made of killed animals? Which ones? How many? Who killed them? What did they do with the rest of the animal?" "Was this stuffed bear alive? Who killed it? Did it have babies?"

Three-and-a-half-year-old Elizabeth found a dead bird outside the door. From prior experience she concluded correctly that it had flown into the picture window and killed itself. She picked it up, said, "Poor birdie," and then, on her way with it to the wooded area at the end of the backyard, added, "It's dead. I'll put it in the woods under the leaves and it'll turn to earth."

Elizabeth was fortunate on many counts. She had obviously been helped by her parents to understand what "dead" means and how we deal with its concrete aspects. They had not burdened and confused her with religious or philosophical explanations, knowing that her young mind could not yet grasp and integrate abstract ideas. She had a chance to learn about death through the common daily experiences with insects, small animals, and plants to which she related matter-of-factly, and which did not touch her personally and arouse painful feelings. She had been fortunate in other ways too. She had not been overstimulated by real or "pretend" experiences in which death involved angry violence or excited hurting and being hurt, and she had been helped to cope with her own early excited–angry hurting impulses by turning them into pity, so that her main feeling response was "Poor birdie." She also had not suffered bereavement or fear for her own life, was spared the very intense feelings that attend such experiences, and could therefore develop a sensible understanding of death that would stand her in good stead later in dealing with more difficult aspects.

In our contemporary Western societies, many young children's experiences with death approximate those of Elizabeth, yet not many children develop as clear and coherent a concept of death. This is mainly due to the fact that so many parents find it so difficult to be in tune with their youngsters' observations and thinking in this area and to talk with them about it at their level of interest and understanding. As with sexual matters, or even more so, parents may not have received help with it from their own parents. They may also have suffered early encounters with death that were too painful to master, or they may fear that any consideration of death will arouse their own and their child's concerns about his and their deaths. For all of us, the fact that death is an inevitable aspect of life remains a fearful and difficult thing to contemplate, one we shy away from, think about only when we have to, and find hard to come to terms with. Parents with young children, in the midst of a period that brims with life, often feel that death has no right to encroach upon them, that they can afford to keep it out of their own minds and can spare their children. This wishful attitude blinds them to the actual frequency of their children's observations of death, to its interesting novelty for them, that they have not yet learned to screen out the way adults often do. However, most parents want to assist their children with all aspects of life and are even willing to include death, when they realize how helpful it is for children to learn about it step by step, starting with ordinary daily experiences, and focusing on the concrete understanding of what "dead" means. Their wish to do well by the child often enables them to overcome their own inner qualms sufficiently to work on the basic concept with him, which will serve as a base for coping with the harder aspects yet to come.

During the later preschool years, children begin to include people they know, as well as themselves, among those who may die, and they struggle to extend their concept of death to "Everyone has to die eventually." In the neighborhood and at nursery school, they hear of the deaths of grandparents, relatives, and pets. In their own families a distant relative may die, or someone Daddy knows at work, or the parents may need to attend a funeral and the children note their sad and upset expressions. All these experiences provide opportunities for further questions and answers, help the child solidify his grasp of death, of its causes, and of how it applies to people: what causes people's deaths, what is a full or an interrupted life span, how we dispose of human dead bodies, and which rites we observe in this connection. These experiences also bring death closer. They touch on the realization that this could happen to my loved ones and even to me. This often causes concern and anguish: "Mommy, how old are people when they die?"; "Mommy, how old are you?"; "Is that very old?"; "Ginny's grandma died. Will our grandma die too?" At times, however, the knowledge of death also provides a content for angry wishes, for "drop dead" thoughts. Mostly these are but dimly imagined or appear in disguised concerns or worries that something will happen to a loved one, but occasionally we hear them verbalized outright: "I hate you. I want you to go away and never come back. I wish you would die!"

No parent enjoys dealing with the children's death-related worries and angers, but many parents manage even this quite well. They do not panic at the child's questions and statements and, without denying mortality, stress that they expect the full life cycle to continue and that premature deaths in others are very unusual: "I am sorry that Mr. X. died. He was very old. He was a grandpa for a long time, and that's when people die." Or, "I am sorry that your friend's dad is dead. It is very unusual for a mommy or daddy to die. Your dad and I expect to live a long time. We will take care of you all along, and when you grow up and have children, we'll enjoy being their grandparents." Or, "your grandma is old but she is not very old, and I expect her to live for a long time. Usually people don't die until they get very, very old." And when they are faced with the child's angry wishes, or with the concerns that arise from them, they may counter with, "Well, people never die because someone wanted it. You and I will go on being alive and well." Likewise, the child's own worry that he may die is put in its proper perspective: "You are very safe and we keep you safe. We expect you to grow up and be a mommy (or daddy) and then a grandma (or grandpa), and perhaps even a great grandma (or grandpa). I know you heard about the little girl who died, but she had a very special, unusual illness, and that's scary and sad, but it's not like the illnesses you get. Most illnesses doctors can help with and people get well again."

The idea that all life eventually ends is best assimilated when it does not present an immediate threat to the child or his loved ones, when real causes are distinguished from imaginary ones, and when it is clear that neither angry feelings nor lack of love as such bring death about (E. Furman, 1978).

During the subsequent years of elementary schooling, these concepts become more fully integrated. As occasions arise, children learn more about the rites we follow when a death happens: the services, the choice between burial and cremation, the ways we express support and sympathy. During this phase in their development, children also begin to think in abstract terms and can add religious or philosophical beliefs to their earlier concrete understanding of death, such as beliefs in the survival of the soul or spirit.

A child's grasp of the basic concrete aspects of death is a prerequisite for coping with a bereavement, that is, with the loss through death of a person with whom he maintained a relationship. When fate confronts young children with such losses before they know at least what "dead" means, it is much harder for them both to learn this concept and to cope with the bereavement.

COPING WITH A BEREAVEMENT

In the course of life we inevitably encounter many losses. We lose money and precious possessions; we may lose parts of our bodies, such as a limb, or parts of our mental self, such as self-esteem; we lose relationships, through temporary or permanent separation, or through emotional withdrawal, or through maturation, such as the loss of the nursing mother at weaning or of the childhood parents during the adolescent transition into adulthood. In spite of some similarities, however, the loss of a loved one through death is unique. It is a truly total and final loss and it carries a special threat to the bereaved by reminding them that they and their other loved ones may die too. When we suffer a bereavement, our minds have to undertake a special mental task in order to master it.

The bereavement task consists essentially of three phases (E. Furman, 1974). The first phase includes understanding and accepting the fact that the loved one is dead, knowing what "dead" means, what the cause of this particular death was, and how and where the bodily remains are disposed of. It also includes coping with the concerns of "Can this happen to me" and assuring oneself that one's own needs will be met, so that life will continue and will be worth living. When these aspects are sufficiently mastered, the next phase unfolds of itself. We call it mourning. It helps us to adjust ourselves to the reality that the deceased is no longer available in the external world. Gradually, as the inner work of mourning proceeds, we enter the last phase in which we resume living without the deceased, in the manner appropriate to our age.

UNDERSTANDING AND ACCEPTING THE DEATH, ITS CAUSES, AND CIRCUMSTANCES

Each bereavement is an individual experience. It happens to individuals whose personalities differ, catches them at different moments in their lives, concerns the loss of very different relationships, and is surrounded by unique circumstances. All this inevitably affects the way in which a person copes with the bereavement task and the extent to which he or she can successfully master it. Children, from their late toddler or early preschool years on, use the same means and can master this difficult task too, if, and only if, their parents can help them with it, as they help them with everything else. The younger the child, the more he needs parental assistance. But adolescents too, and even adults, find it difficult, if not impossible, to mourn alone, without at least the opportunity to share their feelings and to experience the satisfaction of being understood, which makes their remaining relationships and continuing life itself worthwhile. Let us then look more closely at what the bereavement task entails, and how inner and outer factors may help or hinder it.

Children may lose grandparents through death, or older aunts, uncles, and family friends with whom they were close, or pets with whom they shared their daily lives. More often than we realize, they may also experience the death of a friend or schoolmate, a sitter or teacher, or even a sibling. Some of these deaths may have approached slowly and could be anticipated as the children had opportunities to observe the increasing signs of debility caused by sickness and/or old age. Others are sudden, untimely, caused by circumstances which are terrifying in themselves, such as an accident, violence, heart failure, or sudden infant death syndrome. It is helpful when the parents themselves can share the news as soon as possible, let the child know that they will help him with it, and that he will be included in what the family feels and does about it. "I have a very sad thing to tell you. I just found out that grandma died.

That's very hard for all of us. We'll talk about it many times. I want you to understand all about it. We'll stay together and help each other." It is fortunate when the child already knows what "dead" means, or when the parents need only to help him to extend the concept to people ("Do you remember the dead birdie we found? Well, grandma is dead like that birdie.") It is very hard for parents to have to explain concrete death at such a time and for children to begin to learn about it, but it is the first necessary step. At best, all children will review their ideas about death and, over a period of time, at least the younger ones will comment or ask questions as they struggle to get it straight. The days immediately following a death are usually harrying for the whole family as they go through the funeral and observe the rites that accompany it. It is easy to forget about the children at this time or to exclude them in order to spare them hardship, but it is just then that they most need to be kept informed, need to be helped to begin to understand what is happening and why, to share feelings with the family, and to have their support and continuing care and love. Preschoolers are not usually helped by attending all the services, or by viewing the body, although they may manage even that when they do so with a parent who is truly available to them emotionally and able to attend to their needs and questions throughout. They often benefit most from being told what their elders are doing and what is happening to the bodily remains of the deceased, while the child himself perhaps stays at home with a familiar sitter who can also talk with him about it. At a later time, visits to the grave afford another opportunity for the child to see for himself and to integrate his understanding. Older children may prefer to participate directly in all or most of the proceedings with the parents.

Understanding the cause of death is also a part of the initial work. It is often as hard, or harder, than coping with the death itself or with the disposal of the body. It may be a very scary cause, where parents' explanations have to be geared not to further upset the child with gory details, or it may be one that is difficult for youngsters to grasp. For example, children who still think very concretely have interpreted the term *heart attack* as a vicious bodily assault on the patient; they have understood much more readily such wordings as "He had a special sickness inside his body, in a part called the heart. The sickness made his heart not work." However, misunderstandings of the cause of death, as well as of other aspects related to it, arise very often. They can be clarified when the parents appreciate that they not only need to tell their child but also need to listen for his responses, and when they take it for granted that these difficult matters have to be talked over many times before they can be sufficiently mastered.

Adults as well as children need to be clear on all the concrete and particular aspects of the death. Usually adults have access to all the information as a matter of course and are not aware how important this is for them. We come to appreciate it only in the relatively rare instances where we do not know what happened, or cannot understand or accept the cause of death, or where we are uncertain as to what happened to the bodily remains of the deceased: for example, when soldiers are reported missing in action whose deaths cannot be confirmed or bodies returned, or when dead newborns are disposed of by the hospital without the parents' participation in the arrangements and rites. Such circumstances often make it impossible for the family to come to terms and to proceed with the bereavement task. Children, in most instances, do not have access to the necessary information and cannot understand and accept it without parental help. This handicaps many children in coping with their bereavement. One little boy asked over and over "Where is Grandma?" His family thought for a long time that he did not understand, or could not accept, the fact that she was dead, until it became clear that he was quite literally inquiring about where her dead body was, an aspect he had not been told.

Intertwined with the understanding of the facts is the implied threat to the survivor and his need to assure himself of the satisfactory continuity of his own life. Adults as well as children focus on this, and even the special meals and gifts of food that are so often a part of funeral observances are intended to help the survivors partake of the pleasures of meeting their needs and to remind them of the continuing care and love of others. Children approach these concerns in their own ways. Oftentimes they ask, "Can this happen to me, or to you?" They are helped by a reassuring answer: "No, I expect you and us to

live a full long life." But they may also put their questions indirectly, through sudden trivial demands, through insistence
on following the usual routines, and through resenting the disruptions caused by the caring adults' involvement with funeral
arrangements or by their emotional preoccupation with the
death. It may seem selfish, even annoying, but actually contains a very important and necessary question: "Will life still
be worthwhile for me and will you still help make it so?" Instead
of complying with each demand for the sake of reassurance, or
rejecting all of them out of lack of empathy, it helps to do one's
best and to address the real issue in words: "I love you as much
as ever, I'll take care of you as always, and we'll go on doing all
the things together that are fun and that we need to do, even
though grandma died. It's only hard just now. Wait a little
longer and then I'll get your new sneakers (or take you to the
park again, or play a game with you)."

MOURNING

It may take days or weeks before these initial difficult steps
are sufficiently mastered, and misunderstandings and doubts
cleared up, but whenever it is achieved, mourning gets under
way. It is not necessarily marked by an outward show of feelings, by crying or sobbing. Like all internal workings, it may
proceed silently, perceptible perhaps only to the keen, empathic
observer and sharer. Mourning consists of two apparently
opposite processes, detachment and identification.

Detachment is the better known process. It entails the
repeated remembering of life with the deceased, and as each
shared experience is vividly recalled and emotionally relived,
it serves to loosen our bonds with the lost partner in the relationship and gradually to accept reality without him or her.
Memories may come spontaneously or may be triggered by circumstances and events: "Sunday afternoon makes me especially think of grandma, that's when she always used to visit."
"Last time we were here, grandma was with us." Children often remember in actions, rather than words, doing what they
used to do with the deceased. They also rely on using concrete
mementos of the deceased to reexperience life with him or her,

and parents help children by allowing them to keep belongings as well as pictures of the lost loved one. Detachment is known for the intensity and variety of feelings it engenders—longing, pain, anguish, sadness, guilt, anger, helplessness, dejection. Sometimes the feelings are so hard to bear that children feel overwhelmed and need parental comfort, or children may, for the same reason, shy away from their feelings and avoid even thinking about the deceased. This is when, as with all seemingly dangerous feelings, they need the parents' reminders by talking about the dead, by pointing out that everyone has many feelings at such times, and by supporting the child in allowing himself to feel his feelings too. Earlier help in tolerating strong and unpleasant feelings comes in most useful. The greatest obstacle to a child's mourning may come from his parents' difficulty in experiencing their own feelings, because that makes it so hard for them to recognize and support the child's.

The second process, identification, consists of taking into oneself some part of the deceased and making it one's own. In this way we are helped to keep him or her with us always. Adults often take over a dead loved one's interests and activities, or values and attitudes, and enrich their own personalities. Eight-year-old Hal was especially keen on word puzzles and had become very proficient at them over a number of years. It was a hobby that gave him much pleasure, although no other member of his family shared his interest. During his treatment for emotional difficulties, this interest was traced to his relationship with his grandfather, who had often played word games with the boy. The grandfather had died when Hal was barely four years old, but his legacy had become an important part of the grandson's mental makeup.

Sometimes, however, we may also keep within ourselves unhelpful aspects. Some children adopt idiosyncrasies of the deceased or signs of illness they had observed in them, such as, in one case, a stooped gait. When the parents recognized this maladaptive legacy in their four-year-old son Aron, they helped by pointing it out and offering him a better way of coping: "I see you walk like grandpa used to walk. That's really not the way he wanted to walk. It was only part of his being old and ill. It's nice to be like grandpa but I think he'd like you to do some of the things he really enjoyed. Remember how he always fed the birds with you. Perhaps that is something you would like to do too. I'll help you put out a feeder and we can always fill it together, like he did." Aron enjoyed feeding the birds and soon resumed his upright energetic gait.

RESUMING LIVING WITHOUT THE LOST LOVED ONE

Mourning may take a very long time, may never end altogether, but the acute phase passes, and it becomes more intermittent. Once again energy is freed for taking up life's usual routines and activities, and perhaps forming new relationships that will take their place along the memories of the old ones, although they will never actually replace them. This process marks the last phase and mastery of the bereavement task.

Coping with a bereavement is always a long and difficult task, one we wish we could spare ourselves and our children. Sometimes we try to hide the sad news of a death from them, or sidetrack their thoughts about it instead of helping them to understand, or tacitly encourage them to avoid their painful feelings about it, or quickly offer them a substitute relationship in the hope they then won't miss the lost one. Unfortunately it never really works out well. There is no avoiding the hardship. Shortcuts may seem easier at the time, but an unworked-through and unmastered bereavement, like undigested food which remains in the stomach, is bound to cause difficulty in the long run.

WHEN A CHILD'S PARENT DIES

After all we have said about the crucial role of the parent–child relationship, it goes without saying that the death of a parent is the most tragic and traumatic event in a child's life. The child invests so much in the relationship with the parents, and his other relationships are so much less intense, that no relationship between adults can be compared to it. Of course, the younger the child, the more all of his loving and being loved is focused on them, but even for the adolescents the tie with the parents is still their mainstay, and the death of a parent is still the biggest loss.

To the child the parent is not only a loved person, a partner in a relationship. The parent is also a part of the child's own personality. When the parent dies, the child loses a part of himself, the part or parts of his functioning which were still performed by the parent and would have become his own, through their relationship, only in the course of further maturation. The parent would also still have been the one to help his child to cope with the bereavement, and now is not available even to do that.

All the aspects of the bereavement task that we have already discussed apply also to the loss of a parent through death, only more so. Parents of growing children inevitably die untimely deaths and the circumstances surrounding them are always especially frightening and hence difficult to understand and accept. The death of a parent is also a much greater threat to the child's own survival, intensifies the fear of "me next," and immeasurably increases the concerns whether one will be able to go on living and, if so, whether life will still be worthwhile. Likewise, the mourning process is made much more painful and difficult and the deceased parent's support with it is sorely missed. The ultimate resumption of normal living is severely handicapped because, for the developing child, the relationship with the parent is so essential for further growth.

Children, at all ages, therefore, frequently run into difficulties in coping with one or more aspects of the bereavement task. Symptoms and maladjustments of every variety may surface as signs of the unresolved inner struggle, even when their manifest appearance bears no relation to the bereavement. In bereaved children who have undergone psychoanalytic treatment, it was possible to trace the unconscious links between their difficulty in coping with the bereavement and such diverse troubles as eating and sleeping problems, troubles with learning and peer relations, delinquency, fears, and many more. Quite often, however, a child's inability to deal with the loss of a parent becomes evident only years later when he faces the developmental tasks of the next maturational phase and is unable to cope with them: unable, for example, to progress in adolescence following an earlier bereavement during the school years.

Yet many children do master even this most difficult bereavement task when their surviving parent, or familiar parent-substitute, is able to shoulder the almost equally difficult task of assisting them with it. It is sometimes thought that a bereaved and stressed widow or widower cannot take on such a burden, cannot cope with his or her own suffering and help the child with his. But many do, because of the special rewards it entails. Parenting well, doing their best by their child, brings them a great deal of gratification, raises their self-esteem at a time of depletion, and provides solace in sharing feelings. They find that, in bad times as in good ones, the child gives as much to the parent as the parent gives to the child, when they can feel with one another.

WOULD NOT RELIGIOUS BELIEFS HELP TO COMFORT YOUNG CHILDREN AS THEY OFTEN COMFORT ADULTS?

Unfortunately, young children's concrete thinking distorts religious beliefs and tends to make them confusing and frightening rather than comforting. For example, Charlie interpreted the idea of "God took him to live in heaven" so literally that he did not dare venture into the street lest "God" reach down, grab him, and take him away from his parents. Cynthia was scared to go on an airplane because she feared she would remain up in the sky, in "heaven," and never return home. Sean plagued his parents with puzzled questions as to the details of heavenly life: "Are there birthday parties in heaven? Do they have the same candles on cakes? Do they serve spinach?" In several instances children later turned away from religion because it had scared them so when they were little.

The parents' own attitudes also play an important part. Sometimes parents who are not believers themselves offer their young children religious ideas about death in lieu of concrete ones because they hope this will spare them their own doubts and concerns. The children inevitably sense that the parents' feelings are at odds with their words. By contrast, some very religious parents thoughtfully delay religious teachings until their children are of school age, and focus on concrete understanding of death before then, because they want to be sure that religion will not be misconceived and misused, but allowed its rightful place at the right time. Many parents are just uncertain as to how to help their children, uncertain even about their own attitudes to death. When religious concepts are used because "I didn't know what else to say," they are unhelpful. In such instances it is usually more honest and reassuring to deal with the concrete aspects of "dead" first and to answer later questions of belief with "I don't know. Different people believe different things. I have thought about it a lot but I haven't decided yet for myself. It's a hard thing. As you get older and think about it more, maybe you will decide what you want to believe."

WHAT SHOULD PARENTS DO WHEN THEY ARE SO "HUNG UP" ABOUT DEATH THAT THEY JUST CAN'T TALK ABOUT IT OR CAN'T TALK ABOUT IT WITHOUT GETTING ALL UPSET?

Perhaps no parent is always ready to answer questions right away, about this or other difficult topics. If a parent needs time to collect himself, he can tell the child that he will think about his good question and get back to him later. Children wait patiently when they can trust that the parent really will take up the topic with them in time. When parents find that these subjects always upset them very much, it helps them and their child to say, "Look, I find that awfully hard to talk about and I always get upset about it. But that's my trouble and I hope it won't be yours. There are many people who don't get as upset and worried as I do. I am sorry." They may opt for "In the meantime, I'll do my best, but sometimes I'll have to stop and come back to it later, so be patient." Alternatively they may refer the child to the other parent or to another familiar person to talk things over: "It's best you talk to dad (or so-and-so) about this because he doesn't get so upset and will be able to help you better."

It is not shameful for a parent to have trouble with something. It is only unfortunate when he can't acknowledge it and voice the hope that the child will not have to be like him in this respect.

WHAT HAPPENS WHEN INFANTS AND YOUNG TODDLERS ARE BEREAVED, BEFORE THEY CAN UNDERSTAND DEATH?

Insofar as the infant has already had a beginning relationship with the deceased person (perhaps a sibling or grandparent), he will be aware of the loss. Even if he cannot talk yet himself, it will help to tell him that the dead person will not return, to support his feelings and memories, and to assure him that his parents will always return, even when they go away for short periods. Infants are also secondarily affected by the parents' change of mood, preoccupation, and increased absences that are often a part of their response to the bereavement. This can be mitigated when parents keep it in mind and make a special effort not to "forget" their infant and not to overstress his tolerance. In time, as the child gets a little older and learns what "dead" means, he will learn also to apply it to the person he lost but still remembers. It is a difficult task because in these instances "dead" refers to people from the start and is therefore much more threatening.

When infants lose their mothering person through death, it is of utmost importance that she be replaced at once by a preferably already familiar, full-time substitute, who takes over all aspects of parenting, softens the blow of the disrupted relationship, and continues to provide the bodily and emotional care so vital to the distressed baby's survival and development. The understanding of what happened and why will come gradually, with help, as opportunities arise, such as for example, in connection with pictures of the deceased mother, family conversations about her, or anniversaries that sadden the surviving adults and puzzle the child. Often too the child is confronted with the comments of outsiders. For example, eighteen-month-old Molly was raised by her devoted grandmother and father since her mother died shortly after her birth. When grandmother and Molly strolled in the park, other youngsters invariably came up to talk and play with them and commented, "Are you her grandma? Where is her mommy? Why doesn't her mommy take her for a walk?"

It would be a mistake to think that infants are spared hardship. Theirs is often greater, even under optimal circumstances, because they cannot understand and cope at the time, and because, as they get older, they are inevitably prematurely exposed to the fact that people too die. It is not an unmasterable burden but it is a burden. To bear it and to cope with it requires much ongoing help from the surviving parenting figures.

RELATIONSHIPS

Basic Concepts

• Our personalities grow gradually, stage by stage, in innate developmental sequences. Each maturational spurt forms the base for the next stage in growth.

• The child's emotional and educational environment nurtures maturation and helps it to unfold and to achieve its full, harmonious shape at each successive level.

• Relationships make up the child's emotional and educational environment.

• A continuous good enough relationship with a mothering person is crucial to the baby's physical survival, forms the roots of his or her personality, and is the base from which all other relationships grow.

• Through relationships the child learns to care for himself and others.

An Afterthought

Have you asked yourself, as so many have, this question: Why have we talked so much about children's early life and so little about when they are older? Don't many people other than their parents influence their development in those later years, and isn't that part of their development just as important?

When we look at a building we see all its parts above the ground, but not its foundation. We rarely even think about its foundation, and when we do occasionally see it during construction, it appears dull, uninteresting, and unimportant. We can't wait for the "real" building, the upper visible structure, to take shape, so that we will know what it is all about. We forget that the foundation is the most crucial part, that it determines what can be built up and whether what is built on it will hold up.

The child's early years are his foundation, buried and out of view, forgotten by himself and often disregarded by others, along with the raw materials he contributed and the parents' work which helped to mold them together into a coherent whole. The later years, the years of building the visible structure of the personality, are more readily open to view, as are those who participate in giving it its final shape.

We have been looking at what goes on when the foundation is laid.

References

Aichhorn, A. (1925), *Wayward Youth*. New York: Viking Press, 1945.

Barnes, M. J. (1964), Reactions to the death of a mother. *The Psychoanalytic Study of the Child*, 19:334–357. New York: International Universities Press.

Blum, H. P. (1983), Adoptive parents: Generative conflict and generational continuity. *The Psychoanalytic Study of the Child*, 38: 141–163. New Haven, CT: Yale University Press.

Bowlby, J. (1944), 44 juvenile thieves. Their characters and homelife. *Internat. J. Psycho-Anal.*, 25:19–53.

—— (1951), Maternal care and mental health. *Bull. WHO*, 3:355–533.

Burlingham, D. (1952), *Twins: A Study of Three Pairs of Identical Twins*. New York: International Universities Press.

—— (1973), The preoedipal infant-father relationship. *The Psychoanalytic Study of the Child*, 28:23–47. New Haven, CT: Yale University Press.

—— Barron, A. T. (1963), A study of identical twins: Their analytic material compared with existing observation data of their early childhood. *The Psychoanalytic Study of the Child*, 18: 367–423. New York: International Universities Press.

Capote, T. (1965), *In Cold Blood*. New York: New American Library.

Fleming, E. (1974), Lucy. In: *A Child's Parent Dies*, ed. E. Furman. New Haven, CT: Yale University Press, pp. 219–232.

Freud, A. (1946), Freedom from want in early education. In: *The Writings of Anna Freud*, 4:425–441. New York: International Universities Press, 1968.

—— (1947), The establishment of feeding habits. In: *The Writings of Anna Freud*, 4:442–457. New York: International Universities Press, 1968.

——— (1949), Aggression in relation to emotional development. *The Psychoanalytic Study of the Child*, 3/4:37–42. New York: International Universities Press.

——— (1953), Some remarks on infant observation. *The Psychoanalytic Study of the Child*, 8:9–19. New York: International Universities Press.

——— (1958), Adolescence. *The Psychoanalytic Study of the Child*, 13:255–278. New York: International Universities Press.

——— (1963), The concept of developmental lines. *The Psychoanalytic Study of the Child*, 18:245–265. New York: International Universities Press.

Friedlander, K. (1947), *The Psycho-Analytical Approach to Juvenile Delinquency*. New York: International Universities Press.

Furman, E. (1969a), Observations on entry to nursery school. *Bull. Phila. Assn. Psychoanal.*, 19:133–152.

——— (1969b), Some thoughts on the pleasure in working. *Bull. Phila. Assn. Psychoanal.*, 19:4:197–212.

——— (1974), *A Child's Parent Dies*. New Haven, CT: Yale University Press.

——— (1977a), Readiness for kindergarten. In: *What Nursery School Teachers Ask Us About: Psychoanalytic Consultations in Preschools*, ed. E. Furman. Madison, CT: International Universities Press, 1986, pp. 207–233.

——— (1977b), The roles of parents and teachers in the life of the young child. In: *What Nursery School Teachers Ask Us About: Psychoanalytic Consultations in Preschools*, ed. E. Furman. Madison, CT: International Universities Press, 1986, pp. 3–19.

——— (1978), Helping children cope with death. In: *What Nursery School Teachers Ask Us About: Psychoanalytic Consultations in Preschools*, ed. E. Furman. Madison, CT: International Universities Press, 1986, pp. 183–196. Also in: *Young Children*, 1978, 33(4):25–32.

——— (1981a), Children with toddler-like behavior in the nursery school. In: *What Nursery School Teachers Ask Us About: Psychoanalytic Consultations in Preschools*, ed. E. Furman. Madison, CT: International Universities Press, 1986, pp. 149–164. Also Pamphlet Series of the Cleveland Center for Research in Child Development, 2084 Cornell Road, Cleveland, Ohio 44106.

——— (1981b), Treatment-via-the-parent: A case of bereavement. *J. Child Psychother.*, 7:89–101.

——— (1982), Mothers have to be there to be left. *The Psychoanalytic Study of the Child*, 37:15–28. New Haven, CT: Yale University Press.

—— (1983), Something is better than nothing. *Hampstead Bull.*, 6:168–171.

—— (1984), Mothers, toddlers and care. In: *ERIC, ED 256 479*. Urbana, IL: University of Illinois at Urbana-Champaign, 1985. Also Pamphlet Series of the Cleveland Center for Research in Child Development, 2084 Cornell Road, Cleveland, Ohio 44106. Also in: *Preschoolers: Questions and Answers—Psychoanalytic Consultations with Parents, Teachers and Caregivers*. Madison, CT: International Universities Press, 1995, pp. 85–105.

—— (1985a), Learning to feel good about sexual differences. In: *What Nursery School Teachers Ask Us About: Psychoanalytic Consultations in Preschools*. Madison, CT: International Universities Press, 1986, pp. 101–122. Also Pamphlet Series of the Cleveland Center for Research in Child Development, 2084 Cornell Road, Cleveland, Ohio 44106.

—— (1985b), *Play and Work in Early Childhood*. Pamphlet Series of the Cleveland Center for Research in Child Development, 2084 Cornell Road, Cleveland, Ohio 44106. Also in: *Preschoolers: Questions and Answers—Psychoanalytic Consultations with Parents, Teachers and Caregivers*. Madison, CT: International Universities Press, 1995, pp. 3–18.

—— (1987a), *Helping Young Children Grow*. Madison, CT: International Universities Press.

—— (1987b), *The Teacher's Guide to Helping Young Children Grow*. Madison, CT: International Universities Press.

—— (1990), Plant a potato—Learn about life (and death). *Young Children*, 46(1):15–20. Also in: *Preschoolers: Questions and Answers—Psychoanalytic Consultations with Parents, Teachers and Caregivers*, ed. E. Furman. Madison, CT: International Universities Press, 1995, pp. 123–131.

—— (1991), Children of divorce. *Child Anal.*, 2:43–60.

—— (1992a), Thinking about fathers. *Young Children*, 47(4):36–37. Also in: *Preschoolers: Questions and Answers—Psychoanalytic Consultations with Parents, Teachers and Caregivers*, ed. E. Furman. Madison, CT: International Universities Press, 1995, pp. 79–83.

—— (1992b), *Toddlers and Their Mothers*. Madison, CT: International Universities Press.

—— (1993), *Toddlers and Their Mothers: Abridged Version for Parents and Educators*. Madison, CT: International Universities Press.

—— (1994a), Early aspects of mothering: What makes it so hard to be there to be left. *J. Child Psychother.*, 20(2):149–164.

———— (1994b), Learning to enjoy circle time. Pamphlet Series of the Cleveland Center for Research in Child Development, 2084 Cornell Road, Cleveland, Ohio 44106. Also in: *Preschoolers: Questions and Answers: Psychoanalytic Consultations with Parents, Teachers and Caregivers*, ed. E. Furman. Madison, CT: International Universities Press, 1995, pp. 133–145.

———— (1998a), *Needs, Urges, and Feelings in Early Childhood— Helping Young Children Grow*. Madison, CT: International Universities Press.

———— (1998b), *Self-Control and Mastery in Early Childhood—Helping Young Children Grow*. Madison, CT: International Universities Press.

———— Furman, R. A. (1989), Some effects of the one-parent family on personality development. In: *The Problem of Loss and Mourning: Psychoanalytic Perspectives*, ed. D. R. Dietrich. Madison, CT: International Universities Press, pp. 129–157.

Furman, L. (1992), Health professionals and the "Nursing-Working Dilemma." *Zero to Three*, 12:36–37.

———— (1993), Breastfeeding and fulltime maternal employment: Does the baby lose out? *J. Human Lactation*, 9:1–2.

Furman, R. A. (1980), Some vicissitudes of the transition into latency. In: *The Course of Life: Psychoanalytic Contributions Toward Understanding Personality Development*, Vol. 2, ed. S. I. Greenspan & G. H. Pollock. Washington, DC: NIMH, pp. 33–43.

———— (1983), The father-child relationship. In: *What Nursery School Teachers Ask Us About: Psychoanalytic Consultations in Preschools*, ed. E. Furman. Madison, CT: International Universities Press, 1986, pp. 21–34. Also Pamphlet Series of the Cleveland Center for Research in Child Development, 2084 Cornell Road, Cleveland, Ohio 44106.

———— Katan, A. (1969), *The Therapeutic Nursery School*. New York: International Universities Press.

Goldstein, S., & Solnit, A. J. (1984), *Divorce and Your Child*. New Haven, CT: Yale University Press.

Hall, R. (1982), Helping children with speech. In: *What Nursery School Teachers Ask Us About: Psychoanalytic Consultations in Preschools*, ed. E. Furman. Madison, CT: International Universities Press, 1986, pp. 125–126. Also Pamphlet Series of the Cleveland Center for Research in Child Development, 2084 Cornell Road, Cleveland, Ohio 44106.

Krementz, J. (1982), *How It Feels to Be Adopted*. New York: Alfred Knopf.

Menning, B. (1977), *Infertility*. Englewood, NJ: Prentice-Hall.

Provence, S., & Lipton, R. C (1962), *Infants in Institutions: A Comparison of Their Development During the First Year of Life with Family-Reared Infants.* New York: International Universities Press.

Pruett, K. D. (1983), Infants of primary nurturing fathers. *The Psychoanalytic Study of the Child,* 38:257–277. New Haven, CT: Yale University Press.

Schechter, M. (1970), About adoptive parents. In: *Parenthood,* ed. E. J. Anthony & T. Benedek. Boston: Little, Brown, pp. 353–371.

Spitz, R. A. (1945), Hospitalism. An inquiry into the genesis of psychiatric conditions in early childhood. *The Psychoanalytic Study of the Child,* 1:53–74. New York: International Universities Press.

—— (1946), Hospitalism. A follow-up report. *The Psychoanalytic Study of the Child,* 2:113–117. New York: International Universities Press.

Stevenson, O. (1954), The first treasured possession. A study of the part played by specially loved objects and toys in the lives of certain children. With a Preface by D. W. Winnicott. *The Psychoanalytic Study of the Child,* 9:199–217. New York: International Universities Press.

Wallerstein, J., & Kelly, J. (1980), *Surviving the Breakup: How Children and Parents Cope with Divorce.* New York: Basic Books.

Wieder, H. (1977), The family romance fantasies of adopted children. *Psychoanal. Quart.,* 46:185–200.

Winnicott, D. W. (1940), Communication at the Scientific Meeting of the British Psychoanalytical Society. Quoted in: The beginnings and fruition of the self—An essay on D. W. Winnicott by M. Khan, J. A. Davis, & M. E. V. Davis. In: *Scientific Foundations of Pediatrics,* ed. J. A. Davis & J. Dobbing. London: W. B. Saunders Co., 1974, pp. 625–641.

—— (1953), Transitional objects and transitional phenomena. *Internat. J. Psycho-Anal.,* 24:89–97.

Related Reading

A number of publications were referred to in the text and listed in the Reference Section, and a few more are offered for further reading, to amplify or illustrate some of the topics. Some may strike a familiar chord and fit in with your thinking and feeling; others may seem cumbersome or go against the grain. As with all that has been written in this book, you, the reader, will know best which items seem helpful and which to set aside.

Relationships—Infants

Brazelton, T. Berry (1981), *On Becoming a Family*. New York: Delacort Publishers.

Fraiberg, S. (1977), *Every Child's Birthright: In Defense of Mothering*. New York: Basic Books.

Leach, P. (1989), *Your Baby and Child*. New York: Knopf.

—— (1994), *Children First*. New York: Knopf.

Robertson, J., & Robertson, J. (1982), *A Baby in the Family: Loving and Being Loved*. London: Routledge & Kegan Paul.

Tolstoy, L. (1876), *Anna Karenina*. New York: Bantam Books, 1981.

Winnicott, D. W. (1957), *Mother and Child*. New York: Basic Books.

—— (1978), *The Child, the Family, and the Outside World*. New York: Penguin Books.

Relationships—Toddlers

Furman, E. (1992), *Toddlers and Their Mothers*. Madison, CT: International Universities Press.

—— (1993), *Toddlers and Their Mothers: Abridged Version for Parents and Educators*. Madison, CT: International Universities Press.

—— Ed. (1995), *Preschoolers: Questions and Answers—Psychoanalytic Consultations with Parents, Teachers and Caregivers*. Madison, CT: International Universities Press.

Relationships—Preschoolers

Buxbaum, E. (1949), *Your Child Makes Sense*. New York: International Universities Press.

Freud, A. (1949), Nursery school education: Its uses and dangers. In: *The Writings of Anna Freud*, 4:545–559. New York: International Universities Press, 1968.

—— (1962), The emotional and social development of young children. In: *The Writings of Anna Freud*, 5:336–351. New York: International Universities Press, 1969.

Furman, E., Ed. (1986), *What Nursery School Teachers Ask Us About: Psychoanalytic Consultations in Preschools*. Madison, CT: International Universities Press.

—— Ed. (1995), *Preschoolers: Questions and Answers—Psychoanalytic Consultations with Parents, Teachers and Caregivers*. Madison, CT: International Universities Press.

McDonald, M. (1970), Not by the Color of Their Skin: *The Impact of Racial Differences on the Child's Development*. New York: International Universities Press.

Miles, B. (1959), *Having A Friend*. New York: Alfred A. Knopf (a children's book).

Minarik, E. H. (1961), *Little Bear's Visit*. New York: Harper & Brothers (a children's book).

O'Connor, F. (1952), My Oedipus complex. In: *Collected Stories*. New York: Vintage Books, Random House, 1982, pp. 282–291.

Relationships—Schoolchildren

Blos, J. W. (1979), *A Gathering of Days*. New York: Charles Scribner's SMS (a children's book).

Eckert, A. W. (1971), *Incident at Hawk's Hill*. Boston: Little, Brown (a children's book).

Freud, A. (1930), The latency period. In: *The Writings of Anna Freud*, 1:105–120. New York: International Universities Press, 1968.

—— (1952), Answering teachers' questions. In: *The Writings of Anna Freud*, 4:560–568. New York: International Universities Press, 1968.

Simmons, E. (1963), *Mary Changes Her Clothes*. New York: D. McKay Co. (a children's book).

Smith, R. P. (1957), *Where Did You Go? Out. What Did You Do? Nothing*. New York: W. W. Norton.

Index